Endless Inheritance

Endless Inheritance

MOVING FROM FEUDING TO *flourishing*

IN YOUR AFFLUENT FAMILY

RICHARD DEL MONTE

Advantage Media Group is proud to be a part of the Tree Neutral® program. Tree Neutral offsets the number of trees consumed in the production and printing of this book by taking proactive steps such as planting trees in direct proportion to the number of trees used to print books. To learn more about Tree Neutral, please visit **www. treeneutral.com**. To learn more about Advantage's commitment to being a responsible steward of the environment, please visit **www.advantagefamily.com/green**

Advantage Media Group is a publisher of business, self-improvement, and professional development books and online learning. We help entrepreneurs, business leaders, and professionals share their Stories, Passion, and Knowledge to help others Learn & Grow. Do you have a manuscript or book idea that you would like us to consider for publishing? Please visit **advantagefamily.com** or call **1.866.775.1696**.

To my late father, Richard Del Monte, Sr.,
who taught me the true meaning of family,
and to cherish my ancestors, traditions, and heritage.

TABLE OF CONTENTS

INTRODUCTION

I had an inheritance from my father,
It was the moon and the sun.
And though I roam all over the world,
The spending of it's never done.

—ERNEST HEMINGWAY

This book is about inheritance, about the legacy we give our children and grandchildren in this world—both while we are here and when we are gone. I used to believe that inheritance was all about money in the bank, property, and securities, but that was my MBA in financial planning doing the thinking. I've been fortunate enough to see how much good those assets can do, first for the heirs and then for the people and things that matter to them. But I've also seen first-hand how a monetary legacy, no matter how large, is incomplete—and potentially damaging—without a legacy of a different kind.

That second component of inheritance is harder to nail down. You might call it *roots and wings*, or *backbone and funny bone*, or *faith and hope*, or all of the above. It might even be *the moon and the sun* Hemingway refers to. It is a gift you give as a parent that is endless and priceless. It's not a measurable entity. Instead, it's found in the values you give your children; in the way you teach them to love, support, and connect to each other; in how they learn to look beyond themselves and find a way to be a force for good in the world. It's in the memories you share that make them proud to be part of your family, and in the security they find in knowing their family loves, values, trusts, and believes in them. Those are the true components of an endless inheritance.

Ironically, if you leave your family with those intangible but invaluable assets, then you also leave them with the tools they'll need to inherit your wealth and make the most of it.

No matter what you hope and plan to leave the kids in your estate plan, you should know that most inheritance plans don't succeed in the way the giver intended. The money is wasted, or the family fights—or both—in some 70 percent of estate transfers. And in many cases, the larger the estate, the larger the problems it brings.

There is a way to get around the sad and all-too-often devastating fallout that besets not just some, but the majority of families upon the death of their patriarch or matriarch. It has no down side, and it doesn't have to be expensive or all that time consuming. It requires a commitment to do three things: *recognize why most estates fail*; *work on building your own thriving family*; and *apply that new understanding to your family's estate plan*. In the chapters that follow, I'll explain each component and suggest a plan of action. I'll tell you about families that have made costly and painful mistakes, and about families that have grown and thrived.

As for me, I took my first steps toward working as a family wealth coach because of a client who trusted me to protect and grow his life savings into something substantial, maybe even life-changing, for his children to inherit. I was his financial advisor for nearly 20 years, and I thought I was doing a darned good job of it. I'd been able to shepherd his savings through economic good times and bad, guarding his investments so he didn't have to worry.

And then he became ill, and I didn't see him for a few months. Eventually, I got a call from his children, telling me that he had died. I asked if there was anything I could do, as their father's financial advisor, to help the family. And the daughter said, "Yes. We're calling to instruct you to transfer his money to our new investment guy." And then she asked me to issue a check, made out to the man the heirs had chosen to invest their inheritance.

It was a huge red flag, that request to liquidate my client's holdings and sign them over to an individual, because normally if money like that is being transferred, it goes to a trust company or some well-known custodian—like Schwab, or Fidelity, or Merrill Lynch. If I ever asked a client to write a check for the value of his or her life savings payable to "Richard Del Monte," I'd expect to be flat-out denied. Then again, I'd never make that request. Signing over assets to an individual rather than a custodial entity is how people lose their life's savings.

I asked what the heirs intended to do, and was informed that a person they knew, an "advisor," had said he could double their money in 90 days. The investment, he said, was very, very safe.

I couldn't believe my ears. These people were in their 30s and 40s. Did they really think this man was going to snap his fingers and double their father's savings? In 90 days? Without risk? I asked them—begged them, really—to reconsider. *Please don't do this. It's fine if you want to fire me, but at least choose a reputable company. Don't gamble your entire inheritance.* And finally, *I really don't think this is what your father would have wanted.*

But they didn't want to hear it, and so we started the paperwork that would fulfill their wishes. I was shocked, disappointed, and, ultimately, ashamed. All those years, I'd taken care of this man's money, and it had never crossed my mind to ask him how he had prepared his heirs.

I kept coming back to the same question: *What's the point of my whole career if this is what's going to happen after my clients die?*

It was a moment of exceptional clarity, and one that became increasingly important as I began to learn that cases like this are the rule, not the exception. I thought I was serving this family, taking care of them, but I was in a can't-see-the-forest-for-the-trees position. In order to fully serve them, I would have had to take a step back, to see not just the decades I was involved in my client's life, but the larger family, on a longer timeline.

As I took in the gravity of the consequences of such a short-sighted view of financial planning, I looked at every client, and every client's family, with new eyes. I looked at my own family with new perspective as well. *How can I prepare them?* I thought. *How can I keep this from happening to the people who entrust their wealth to me? And to the people I care about?*

My experience with this one client's investment account had a huge impact on me, both professionally and personally.

I studied the grim facts about the vast majority of family wealth being frittered away by the children who inherit it. I read one account after another of families irrevocably broken by their wealth and their battles over inheritance. I studied family dynamics, conflict resolution, and what it takes for an affluent family to be cohesive and stay whole, both in the here and now, and when the parents pass away and leave the rising generation, ready or not, in control of their worldly goods. I looked high and low for successful families and the advisors who were helping them. I became a Certified Wealth Consultant with The Heritage Institute and dedicated years of my career to understanding and implementing the practices of the best and brightest minds in the business. I eventually became a faculty member at the Institute for Preparing Heirs, and a founding member of the Council for Shared Leadership—the organization that has defined the fundamentals of excellence for values-based family advisors.

It's in the work of coaching families and helping them rethink the ways they relate to one another and to inheritance that I've found my calling. There are days when I think I might have done more for a family's long-term financial outlook in one family meeting than I could have accomplished in years of investment advising. After all, what's the point of accumulating and investing wealth if it is destined to be squandered—or worse, to ruin the lives of the people you care about most in the world?

I'm sharing my experience and some of our solutions in these pages because I believe that every family can be a thriving family; that every family can find a way to better prepare their children for the privileges and responsibilities that come with significant wealth. I hope you will find this book helpful in creating your personal *moon and sun*—the endless inheritance that only you can give your family.

—RICHARD DEL MONTE

part one

SHIRTSLEEVES TO SHIRTSLEEVES

CHAPTER 1

The Risks Families Face

Years ago, travel and restaurant magnate Curtis Carlson was interviewed for a *Fortune* magazine article about inheritance issues. Carlson, who built his $700 million fortune from scratch, made no bones about the one thing that gnawed at him when it came to his remarkable, self-made success: "There's nothing people like me worry about more," he said, than "how the hell do we keep our money from destroying our kids?"

It sounds crazy to work all your life for something and then to spend your sleepless nights worrying about the damage it might do, but Carlson's fears were well founded. The fact is, there are a multitude of widespread problems associated with raising children in wealthy families and with the transfer of wealth from one generation to the next. One recent study found that more than 40 percent of high-net-worth individuals have personally experienced family wealth leading to conflict. The research also revealed that the greater the wealth, the more likelihood there was of conflict. So a $700 million estate might be good cause to give a man worry for his daughters' well-being.

Anecdotally, we've all heard stories of families and fortunes devastated by the excesses of wealth—the Woolworth heiress who squandered a fortune that would be worth half a billion dollars today; the heir to the A&P grocery fortune who blew through a $100 million inheritance and died bankrupt; the Johnson family heiress who lived a widely publicized life of fame-seeking excess and drug addiction, then heartbreakingly died at just 30 years old; the heirs to the Orkin fortune locked in a web of lawsuits over trust distributions that have made enemies of brothers and sisters, husbands and wives, parents and children for years now—with no end in sight.

In terms of sheer waste, consider the case of one of the wealthiest Americans in history, Cornelius Vanderbilt, who left an estate worth upward of $167 billion in today's dollars when he died in 1877. He left most of his estate to one son, with the rest divided among his eight daughters, his wife, and charities. Four of Vanderbilt's children contested the will, and one ultimately committed suicide over the escalating feud that followed. In the decades that followed, Vanderbilt heirs spent shamelessly and with what one economist referred to as "unparalleled self-gratification and . . . downright stupidity." The press took to referring to "The Fall of the House of Vanderbilt" as the family became increasingly known not for its business enterprises, but for its lavish estates, hedonistic parties, and romantic scandals. The extraordinary Vanderbilt fortune was scattered in the wind.

Was it the inherited wealth that brought these families to ruin and waste? There's no denying that the money acted as an accelerant for problems that were already smoldering in each case—intensifying a lack of judgment, an unfortunate affinity for extravagance, a slip into substance abuse, a family rift, a void created by feeling unfulfilled, or economic "stupidity" into situations much bigger and much more harrowing.

But for every tragic case of inherited wealth, you can find a less-publicized but very much opposite story—the antidote, if you will. These are the stories of heirs who went on to do great things through the empowerment of family wealth. Consider the heirs of upstate New York investor and businessman John Andrus, who honor their patriarch's wishes to use his wealth to provide "opportunities for youth and rest for old age" today, just as they have for five generations. Their Surdna Foundation, which manages nearly a billion dollars in assets, is just one of a number of family philanthropies. In fact, the family specifically targets each new generation with giving opportunities of its own, in the hopes, no doubt, of giving them a shared mission, and of instilling an association between wealth and social responsibility.

In another example of great wealth put to great use, Europe's Rothschild family, with a fortune so vast they once bailed out the English economy, has used a combination of family awareness, mentoring, philanthropy, and education about finance to keep not only the fortune but the family intact for more than 200 years and counting.

What's the biggest difference between the families with disastrous inheritance experiences and those that have flourished? Both sets of families acquired great wealth. Both invested a great deal of time and trouble in estate planning. But the families that kept their wealth, the ones that still celebrate their shared history and continue to work together, didn't just prepare their money to pass it to their heirs; *they prepared their heirs to receive the money.* And in so doing, they found a way to keep the family unified, strong, and prosperous for generations.

A CRISIS OF EPIC PROPORTIONS

I'd like to tell you that the tales of waste and loss and destruction of family fortunes are the exception. We'd all like to believe that. I'd like to tell you each family that came to a dreadful end made some grand failure—didn't plan or spoiled their kids or invested without caution, too. But none of these things are true.

The fact is, inheritance loss and the fallout for families are the reality for the majority of estates—not just for the few. How big are the failings in the transfer of wealth? Frankly, they're staggering. In a landmark study by Roy Williams and Vic Preisser that spanned more than 20 years and followed 3,250 affluent families who transferred wealth, *70 percent* of families failed at passing on wealth through the second generation. Failure, in the world of multigenerational wealth planning, means the offspring either squandered all the money or they wound up fighting with or suing each other, destroying the family's harmony.

To make matters worse, that 70 percent loss rate is compounded with each generation, so if your kids wind up being among the lucky minority who preserve your wealth after your death, the 70 percent loss rate kicks in again when your grandchildren inherit—at which point over 90 percent of estates are lost. *Ninety* percent. Think about that: There is a 90 percent chance your great-grandkids will never see a dime of the wealth you amassed.

The statistics apply to vast amounts of money just as well as they do more modest fortunes, and lest there be any confusion, these are not cases of family wealth being spread more thinly over multiple generations of an ever-growing, flourishing family—that would be much easier to live with. These are cases of catastrophic loss, of families torn apart, of failure—not dissemination. This phenomenon transpires across all levels of wealth, and in countries all over the world. It happens whether there are high estate taxes in the home country or none. It happens whether the family had an elaborate estate plan in place—or didn't bother.

The failure of wealth transfer, as it turns out, is so common there's a centuries-old adage to describe it: *Shirtsleeves to shirtsleeves in three generations.* And that adage has counterparts in cultures all over the world. In China, it's *rice paddy to rice paddy.* In Ireland: *clogs to clogs.* In Italy, a rather poetic version translates to: *from stalls to stars to stalls again.*

This is a crisis of epic proportions, and yet, I challenge you to ask anyone you know if they think this fate might befall their own family—and the vast majority will answer: *No.* Even if *they know* that 70 percent of estates will be lost in the first inheriting generation—even when tens or hundreds of millions of dollars are involved. Even if *they know* that in far too many cases, siblings and cousins and parents and children will turn on each other in anger and frustration, saying and doing things that will impact the family for generations. Even then, you'll be hard-pressed to find a family leader who is mindful enough to nod and acknowledge: *Yes. This could happen to me. What can I do to prevent it?*

My team and I have seen this denial time and time again. When we conducted an informal survey of 20 heads of affluent families in their seventies, they *all*—100 percent—thought their estate plans were going to be successful. When asked why, their answers were almost identical. They all said, using slightly different terms: "My kids get along great, and I've left instructions in my trust for how I want my affairs handled, so I'm fine." Even when they were made aware of the 70 percent failure statistic, nobody blinked.

I wish each of those families—and every family, for that matter—success in their estate transfer. But I've been doing this work far too long to believe even for one minute that all 20 families are going to get through it unscarred and unbroken—or that the fortunes they worked their lives for will be even partially preserved for the next generation, or the one after that. Successful estate transfer doesn't just happen. Without a realistic and deliberate intervention to change the odds, many of those families will join the legions of others who perpetuate the *shirtsleeves to shirtsleeves* adage in the United States and around the world.

ARE TRADITIONAL ADVISORS TURNING A BLIND EYE?

It would be convenient if we could explain away the incredible statistics about lost wealth by laying them at the feet of financial and legal advisors. If the money was poorly invested, or eaten up by taxes, or even stolen away by a shady investment guru, at least we could understand what happened—and maybe try to avoid the same through steps as simple as reference checks or use of a diverse group of advisors.

The fact is, though, of all the failed estates in the Williams and Preisser study, fewer than 5 percent were caused by financial, estate, or tax planning errors. The study revealed that traditional financial and estate planning professional communities are performing their jobs extremely well—at least in the sense that they're taking care of the money entrusted to them, and making sure it successfully makes it into the next generation's hands with a minimum of estate transfer costs and delays.

Despite their high competence in these areas, however, many inheritance planning professionals are failing in another way. In any other field with the kinds of predictably ineffective outcomes we see in estate transfer, the relevant professionals find a way to address the problem—or at least to try. But these well-meaning legal and financial advisors are either not seeing the big picture regarding the fate of the treasures they're charged to protect—or they are ill-equipped to handle it. The majority has no methodology for addressing this problem—not the tools, the time, or the motivation. They do what they can with legal structures—controlling trusts and conditional estate transfer plans—but, as we'll see in the next chapter, these often become part of the problem, not part of the solution. And so this cycle of fortunes made and lost persists across generations, centuries, cultures, and nations.

A CAUSE CLOSER TO HOME

In 95 percent of the failed wealth transfer cases investigated by Williams and Preisser, the crux of the problem came from within the family. In all too many cases, a lack of communication or trust derailed even meticulously laid estate plans. In others, the rising generation was simply unprepared or unwilling to manage their inheritance responsibly. In some, a lack of a shared vision or mission among the family members got in the way. Often, two or more of these issues overlapped, creating more potential not just for lost wealth, but also for family strife.

Given these facts, some family leaders and their advisors just look the other way—choosing complacency. Please don't take this path. This happens to good families all the time, not just families with spoiled or troubled children; not just families with fractured relationships; not just families that are easy to dismiss as somehow setting themselves up for a fall. It happens in families that get along, that have a high level of education, that seem rock solid. It happens in families like yours and mine. In fact, statistically speaking, it is a virtual certainty that your family's fortune will not escape this terrible fate unless you do something to prevent it.

In light of the gloomy outlook of inheritance transfer and some very disturbing but anecdotal evidence of kids ruined by their parents' wealth, some of the wealthiest parents in the world have announced that money ruins families, and that they are leaving their wealth to charity. It's easy enough to think they may be right—just one look at the shameless Rich Kids of Instagram sharing pictures of themselves guzzling champagne on private jets or passed out in their Bentleys and Lamborghinis is enough to scare any parent half to death. But money does *not* have to be a destructive force. It is *not* a fact that money ruins kids. That is nothing more than a very limiting and unfounded belief.

While it is true that leaving wealth to unprepared heirs can put them—and their inheritance—at great risk, there is absolutely no reason that even great wealth left to heirs who have been well prepared has to be harmful. On the contrary, well-prepared heirs have the very same opportunities for living happy and productive lives that their wealth-creator parents enjoy. For this very small but fortunate cadre of heirs, wealth can be a huge blessing, both to them and to the causes and concerns they care about most.

Every one of the issues that is responsible for so much heartbreak and loss in families—ineffective and toxic communication, lack of trust, unpreparedness, absence of goals and ideals—can be addressed. These are fundamental matters that deserve the time and attention of parents, children, and grandchildren. It is never too soon, or too late, to start preparing the rising generation of your family—not just to inherit whatever worldly goods you plan to leave them, but also to be engaged and contributing members of the family who value and respect each other, appreciate their family history, and are able to handle the responsibilities and privileges that come with wealth. These skills are the keys to getting on track for a successful estate transfer in the future, but they're also the keys to having a thriving family life in the here and now.

— *Exercise* —

PICTURE THE POSSIBILITIES

Taking a step back can be an invaluable tool in gaining perspective, but, sometimes, looking ahead can be just as illuminating. Do you think your family is immune to the prospect of being damaged by the toxic effects of wealth? Will they be able to continue your family's history of making a significant difference in the world? Are they prepared for a financial inheritance? Take a minute to work through this exercise about the possibilities for your family's future:

Imagine your family 60 years from now, getting together for a picnic at a place they used to visit with you. Write down your greatest wishes for what's happening on that day:

- Who is there?

- What are they talking about?

- What are they doing? Cooking? Playing games? Taking a walk? Laughing together?

- How are your children, grandchildren, nieces, and nephews interacting with each other?

- What kind of people are they?

- What are their own families like?

- How do they interact with their partners and/or children?

- What shared memories do they talk about?

- Are they happy? Connected? Fulfilled?

- What is going on in each of their lives?

- How are they making a difference in the world?

- As you watch your family, what do you feel most grateful for?

- What do you wish you could say to them?

With your answers to this exercise in mind, consider this: What is your current estate plan doing to foster your vision and make it real? What are you doing today, and what will you do as you move forward, to make your hopes and dreams for your family's future a reality?

CHAPTER 2

Inheritance-Planning Mistakes

The first step in successful inheritance planning is acknowledging the common mistakes that cause estate transfers to fail. Most of these mistakes boil down to heirs who aren't prepared to inherit—not to any failures in the estate plan itself. You might think of optimum inheritance planning as a platform with three legs: the first is *financial planning,* which grows and protects the money; the second is *estate planning,* which prepares the money for the heirs; and the third is *preparing the heirs*—not just to receive their inheritance, but also to effectively communicate, get along, and be supportive of one another.

Everyone knows the first two legs are essential—but the third is easily overlooked. It might be convenient to think that last leg takes care of itself, or that the responsibility falls to the heirs to handle when the time comes, but neither of those things is true.

Consider this true story of a family that learned this lesson the hard way: A middle-aged man—an architect—went to his family's estate attorney and announced that his father had been diagnosed with a terminal illness. The father had built an estate worth more than $12 million, and he wanted to complete his estate planning immediately.

The architect explained his parents' wishes for provisions for the five adult children. The architect and one other sibling were successful in business and financially independent, so the parents wanted to establish trusts the two could access upon retirement. The other siblings, though, had struggled over the years. They'd spent extravagantly, made regrettable career and business decisions, and endured painful and costly divorces. The parents had purchased a home for each of these children to give them some stability, and to ensure the three would be financially secure, the parents wanted to transfer a large sum of money to each when they passed on.

Everyone involved had agreed to these provisions, and the architect asked that the estate documents be prepared right away. From a legal and financial standpoint, this was a well-thought-out, carefully crafted application of traditional estate planning, in compliance with the highest standards of the industry.

Just a week after the documents were signed, the architect's mother died. Six days later, his father passed away as well—his life expectancy of a few years reduced to just weeks by his grief. An entire generation of the family was gone.

The estate plan had come full circle, from planning to implementation, in just a few weeks, and the attorney was satisfied with his work—everything that could have been done to help the family minimize taxes and pass their wealth to their children had been done, and in record time.

But was it all really a success? After two years, the architect returned. His family was in crisis. The three siblings who'd been in financial trouble to begin with had spent every penny of their inheritance. Worse, all three homes—the parents' insurance that their offspring would always have a place to live—were mortgaged to the hilt. There was nothing left—not to pay for college for the grandchildren, not to cover the steep new mortgage payments, nothing.

The now-panicked three had turned to the two siblings with their inheritance in trusts, demanding to be rescued from the mess they'd created. The architect was angry and heartbroken. He knew that any money he gave them would just evaporate—millions of dollars were already gone. What had happened to his family? Why couldn't his siblings manage their own affairs? How could he help them when they were so foolish with money? In 24 months, they had blown through the assets their parents worked 50 years to build. And the family unity the mother and father had wanted above all else had been wiped out along with the money.

The "textbook" estate plan had accomplished exactly what it was designed to do: transfer the greatest amount of wealth, with the smallest possible tax liability, to the heirs. But it had also led to a squandered fortune and a bitter, broken family.

What went wrong? Was it inevitable that the spendthrift siblings would waste their inheritance? Could their parents have done anything differently—apart from raising all five children again to be smarter about money—to achieve a better outcome?

A gut reaction to the problems this family experienced might be that they needed more restrictive trusts, but in my experience—and research bears it out—those almost never solve inheritance problems. Ironically, they only serve to exacerbate them. Children with no financial skills and terrible spending habits will either blow through the money soon after it reaches them, or enlist the help of all-too-willing attorneys to break the trusts. Along the way to getting their hands on their inheritance one way or another, they frequently clash with siblings and other family members, and often develop deep and abiding resentments toward the parents who created the restrictions in the first place.

The parents could have prevented the financial devastation of three of their children and the ensuing family rift by taking the time to prepare their heirs to be cooperative, collaborative, and financially competent. Yes, that is a tall order, but it was absolutely, inarguably possible.

AN ALL TOO COMMON PROBLEM

In my years of experience, first in financial advising and then in family coaching, I've seen countless "good" estate plans disintegrate the moment the assets began to flow through the fingers of unprepared heirs. I have worked with thousands of families, from the moderately wealthy to some of the richest in America. Time and again, I see children of all ages who were never taught an appropriate or healthy understanding of money, never taught to work cooperatively, never taught how to work through a logistically and emotionally complicated challenge like an estate transfer. I've seen families in which rifts between siblings or children and parents have been allowed to linger for years and even decades—and families like the architect's, ripped to shreds as they battle over estates.

These are the key mistakes families are making:

Mistake #1: Poorly Prepared Heirs

Unprepared heirs destroy virtually all estate plans they touch and are a direct cause of the apathy and lack of motivation known as *affluenza* and of much unhappiness in families. This is the primary issue that rendered the estate plan for the architect's family not just ineffective, but damaging, in the long term.

In the Williams and Preisser study, 25 percent of estate transfer failures could be chalked up to parents' failure to prepare their heirs for the roles and responsibilities they would assume after inheriting. The heirs who fall into this category range from the completely unequipped to those who are lacking just a few key element of readiness.

On one end of the spectrum are heirs who've been raised with no real sense of the value of money or what it can accomplish when put to its highest and best use. Many have acquired the compounding problem of consumerism—leading lives of conspicuous consumption and never footing—or even seeing—the bills for their excess. These spoiled heirs can be challenging to guide. Fortunately, they are also a small minority.

Next are the children—whether they're 18 or 58—who've never been taught the basic principles of budgeting, saving, or managing household expenses—let alone anything about the intricacies of investments. Like the architect's siblings, these heirs have no experience managing their own affairs and monetary responsibilities. Many have been bailed out time and again by their parents.

Another surprisingly large group of unprepared heirs have no idea of the family wealth—that it even exists, let alone that they will one day be responsible for it. It's remarkable how often this happens. Parents are often uncomfortable talking about money with their families, and so some just don't, and even choose to raise their kids with no knowledge of it, believing it will help them be more grounded, motivated, and responsible. The end result is heirs who are eventually blindsided by inheritance—and decidedly not always elated or empowered by the news. Some are shocked. Some are confused, not knowing how sudden wealth redefines them. Some feel guilt, unworthiness, and even shame because of it. Some act rashly and spend the money away in a heartbeat. Some even give it all away to unburden themselves.

Some heirs know they will inherit, but have no understanding of the implications when a bequest consists of real estate, family business ventures and securities—but not cash. ("But where is the *real* money?" is one of the most common things attorneys hear during the estate settlement process.) Other children inherit treasured objects, collections, leases—even working farms and live animals—without knowing anything about the care and maintenance of those possessions. Some are financially bright, but have no understanding of how to work cooperatively with others in the new relationships that are thrust on them. For example, becoming a trustee, beneficiary, co-owner of real estate assets, or member of the board of directors of a family business—with no advanced training—is a recipe for disaster.

No one is born knowing how to manage and protect millions, or even billions, of dollars in assets, but nearly every heir can become emotionally and intellectually capable of the job with the right preparation. Without it, many are so emotionally and intellectually unprepared that they behave like lottery winners, who not coincidentally, share that 70 percent loss of wealth statistic. Actually, estimates suggest most lottery winners lose their windfalls within a few years—even more quickly than the generational loss of inherited wealth.

What happens to unprepared recipients of windfall wealth? Often, the ready availability of large amounts of money exacerbates whatever issues the inheritor already has. A mathematical mind and drive to preserve the family legacy, for example, might lead to a deep involvement in investment strategizing. A desire to save the world might lead to critical donations or the creation of a foundation. On the other hand, a habit of dabbling in drugs might explode into a full-blown addiction. A flighty heir who might once have been quick to quit a job or make an impulse purchase might become dangerously enabled. And an heir who's always been a little insecure or gullible can become an easy target for grifters and con artists.

For better or worse, money is a powerful accelerant for whatever's already going on at the core of a person's life. How much greater a gift will you be leaving your children if you first ensure they are prepared to receive it and use it well?

Mistake #2: Lack of Communication

Lack of preparedness and lack of communication go hand in hand, and both are factors in many—if not most—estate failures. Whether the breakdown is between spouses, between parent and child, among the children, or all of the above, the outcome is the same: estate plans that are doomed to fall apart when questions and conflicts arise and it's too late to seek guidance or clarification from the source—the parents or other wealth creators. These are issues that need to be addressed now, while the whole family is intact and mom and dad maintain enough influence to help facilitate.

According to a 2014 study by UBS investment banking company, while 83 percent of parents surveyed had a current will, only 50 percent had discussed inheritance plans with their children. And only 34 percent had revealed their wealth to their heirs. This is the simplest failure to correct in estate planning—speaking openly with your children about your intentions, taking questions, working through any concerns that arise as a result of those conversations. If you find it too stressful, hire a facilitator to help you keep things on track and avoid squabbles.

All too often, estate and financial planning professionals have a front row seat for the fallout of this lack of communication. Any one of us can tell you that some of the most painful and damaging of these situations are the result of estates that are divided unequally—often for sound, fair, and perfectly logical reasons—and heirs who don't understand or won't accept the provisions as they were designed. I've seen this so many times—perhaps one child was lent a large sum of money while a parent was alive, and that sum has been deducted from his or her inheritance. Or perhaps a sibling feels that such a deduction should have been made. Perhaps one child moves home and helps tend to the day-to-day needs of an aging parent, then feels that altruism should have been reflected in the will. These conflicts—even over small bequests, let alone large estates—can lead directly to families losing decades of connectedness and even to relationships so broken that siblings never speak to one another again.

In my own family, we have a well-known instance of this kind of split. During the 1940s, my grandfather and his sister fell out about a small disputed bequest (a shotgun) in their father's will. In the aftermath, they didn't speak to each other for more than two decades. I knew both of these people well, and they were both kind and loving—but neither could ever get past the deep rift that had been caused by their disagreement. When my grandfather was on his deathbed, his sister was moved to try to bury the hatchet, and came to the hospital to say goodbye. He was told by his children that his sister was in the lobby and asking to see him. His answer? I'm sorry to say, it was, "Tell her to go to hell." Family lore suggests those were his last words.

How sad is that?

How much better would it have been for their father to have sat down with them together and told them what he wanted and why? He could have listened to their concerns, helped them work through whatever the root of this problem was (which was no doubt more deep-seated than the inheritance itself), and allowed them to move forward after his death without all that anger and bitterness tainting the rest of their lives.

Disagreements like this are all too common in families. They can occur at any time—not just in inheritance situations. Why are they allowed to fester and divide families into warring factions for years—or even decades? In some cases, people just don't know how to communicate effectively with each other. They've never learned how to have a dialogue that's truly about creating peaceful solutions rather than about establishing who is right and who is wrong. They don't know how to step outside of themselves, even for just a moment, to try to understand how the other party feels. In other cases, people just don't have the stomach for the difficult, sad, and sometimes scary conversations that might require them to be vulnerable, or repentant, or forgiving. Some have been so hurt they're terrified of trusting again. And so they stay away, and at odds, indefinitely.

Mistake #3: Lack of Trust

The root cause of countless estate failures lies in a fundamental lack of trust between parents and children, between siblings, and even between family advisors and heirs. The most basic tenets of trust are simple: Each person intends to, is capable of, and will commit to fulfilling his or her obligations to the others. These obligations come in all shapes and sizes, from the relatively small to the truly daunting: showing up as promised at a family event; honoring a commitment to stop haranguing a family member about grooming or personal habits; delivering on a pledge to work harder at school or hold a job; swearing to get professional help to deal with alcoholism.

Over time, the ways we fulfill, or neglect, these obligations become part of our relationships with one another. We learn to trust or distrust the people we love based not just on whether they are trustworthy, but also whether we ourselves are trustworthy. If a family is built on relationships where there is no trust, then its members are destined to struggle to connect, to enjoy one another's company, and ultimately, to survive the trial of an estate transfer without falling out. Trust issues are far better dealt with before such a true test arrives.

In many estate transfers, trust issues come to the fore based on the roles members of the rising generation are asked to play. Choosing one child as executor or trustee with responsibility over the others can be a blueprint for disaster—especially if you choose a child who is not fully trusted by the siblings. Designating a trustee who is not fully cognizant and capable of the responsibilities of the job also sows the seeds for failed trust.

Another all-too-common manifestation of lack of trust is, ironically, reliance on restrictive provisions in estate planning documents—legal trusts. These tools are designed to exert control over heirs by limiting their access to inherited wealth after the parents have passed away. These legal maneuvers may limit trust distributions or other bequests based on the heirs' age, life milestones, income, "provable" responsibility, or any number of arbitrary measures.

Unfortunately, these kinds of restrictions—especially coupled with a lack of communication and information about them ahead of time—almost always breed resentment. One heir to a highly restrictive trust once tearfully told me, "I went my whole life believing my parents trusted me and believed in me. My memory of our great relationship is tainted by this, their final message to me."

Furthermore, restrictive trusts that distribute assets based on age can actually foster entitlement. These heirs simply become "waiters," as in waiting for their inheritance. Rarely do they pull their lives together in the way their parents think they might by, say, age 30.

Nobody wants to be controlled from the grave. Relying on trustees (who are often strangers to the heirs) and legal maneuvers puts trust outside the family rather than keeping it within—and as a result, the measures that may reassure parents in their lifetimes can ultimately hurt their heirs and the entire family.

Mistake #4: Lack of Mission and Vision

The last large-scale reason for estate failures cited in the Williams-Preisser study is a lack of agreed-upon purpose for wealth. If an estate consists of wealth beyond what the heirs need to take care of themselves, then what becomes of the rest? Families who don't think about this issue, discuss it, and plan for it, tend to go their separate ways, and often the wealth ends up squandered. With no coordination or cohesive strategy, everybody does their own thing, and we often see cases where it becomes a race to spend for some heirs as they buy sports cars or planes and participate in other extravagant consumption. And here is where you find the "shirtsleeves" proverb fulfilling itself in spades.

Of course, lack of a shared vision can be subtle and difficult to nail down. Quite often, it's a shadow factor in failed estates—a family that finds it has no way to move forward after a death in the family, but doesn't quite know why.

Consider the case of the Summerfields, a family I knew and once talked with about helping to prepare their rising generation for the transfer of wealth from the parents. The parents had done a wonderful job of building a successful and cooperative family. The three children were close and communication was strong among all five family members. The parents felt confident that after they passed on, the kids weren't going to fight or fall apart.

But there were a number of missing pieces, including the fact that these kids—young adults—didn't understand their parents' vision for the family's wealth—and in fact had very different intentions for it and no agreement even among themselves. They had no experience working together on something as crucial as stewarding a large estate. And in one way, they were like the architect's siblings: they didn't know the first thing about investments, taxes, or trusts.

Even though everybody got along "just fine," the Summerfields' estate planning was a calamity in the making. The father passed away first, and then the mother a couple years later. The kids were together with her when she died on a Friday. On Monday, they held the funeral. On Tuesday, they met the estate attorney to review the will. But by the end of that meeting, the child who'd been appointed executor had resigned, and all three siblings agreed to hire their own attorneys and communicate through them going forward. The enormity of the responsibility, compounded by their grief and the issues they hadn't considered, had driven them apart.

I lost track of the Summerfields after their falling out, but I'd like to think they were able to find a way to salvage their relationships with one another. I firmly believe, though, that if the family had worked together ahead of time to create a shared mission for their wealth, if they'd prepared the children to inherit, then they could have navigated a way through that terrible Tuesday meeting and gotten on with grieving their mother's death and supporting one another.

ALL HOPELESS CASES?

Looking at the estate failures of other families is a sobering, humbling and deeply discouraging business. I'm sometimes asked if it's simply the destiny of wealthy families to know their children will squander fortunes and squabble with each other for want of a better path to the next generation. And the answer is, *Of course not*. There is always another way.

Even as you read these pages, there are families thinking their estate transfers through and preparing their heirs to be successful throughout the process. Inherited wealth can be a powerful force for good in the lives of your children, grandchildren, and great-grandchildren. In order to harness that power, it's time to take a long and clear look at how to create a legacy that extends beyond money or property to encompass all the tools your family needs to thrive.

In the next chapter, we'll examine what a thriving family looks like, and prepare to take steps to help your family become one.

—— *Exercise* ——

TOUGH QUESTIONS

None of us wants to think about our own mortality, and perhaps the legal aspects of your estate plan are already in place and you're satisfied with what's been done. It may be easy to imagine your family working cooperatively and capably through an estate transfer—or alternately, it may be so impossible to imagine, you don't even want to try. No matter where your family's estate plan stands, though, I urge you to ask yourself the questions below.

Write down your answers to these inheritance-related questions about your children (or grandchildren, nieces, nephews, and other heirs) ages 15 and older. Be honest— even critical—in your responses:

1. How will your children handle your estate when you're gone?

2. How much do your children know about what they are or aren't going to inherit?

3. How much do your children know about your hopes and aspirations for how they'll utilize their inheritance?

4. Do your children talk about your estate as if it already belongs to them?

5. How much experience do your children have managing smaller or finite amounts of money? (Have they made a budget and tried to stick to it? Have they planned for a long-term financial goal, perhaps by having to wait, save, and/or work for something they couldn't have right away?)

6. How much financial support do you currently provide to your adult children?

7. How much understanding do your heirs have about basic financial literacy concepts like investments, compound interest, and taxation? How much experience have they had making decisions about any of these? How much experience have they had working together cooperatively in these matters?

8. Describe the quality and effectiveness of your children's current relationships with your trusted financial and legal advisors.

9. How well do your children communicate with one another—and do they do so respectfully and positively?

10. How effective are they at solving disagreements between themselves without outside intervention?

11. Among themselves, what specific roles do your children play—like leader, peacemaker, trouble-maker? Have they shown the ability to rise above those roles when it's necessary?

12. Do your children trust each other?

13. How free is your family of any lingering or unresolved resentments, especially among your children, that might resurface one day and be a source of conflict?

14. How aware are your children about where your wealth comes from and what it took to achieve it?

15. Are your children proud of their family name and family history?

16. How much do your children appreciate the power of money to better the lives of others?

17. In what ways have your children been successful in finding fulfillment in their own lives?

18. Do you have a family continuity plan that goes beyond the next generation?

When you've answered all the questions, look back at your responses. If you are completely at peace with your answers, then you may well have already done the work that's needed to help your family successfully inherit. If you have responses you are not pleased with, it's time to start addressing these issues within your family.

CHAPTER 3

A Place of Possibility

As a family wealth transfer coach, I help families discover where the discrepancies are between that future they imagine and the one that's likely to materialize if family dynamics continue on their current path. What it's really about is bringing people from a place of resignation or status quo to a place that is proactive in creating and healing relationships. It's about moving families away from their limitations and toward a more open, creative, can-do place—a place of possibility.

I'd like to tell you about two families to illustrate the power of this place:

A TALE OF TWO FAMILIES

Some time ago, I got a phone call from a man who was worried about his son. The boy was about to turn 18, and at that milestone he was going to inherit a $30 million trust fund from his grandfather.

Does it sound like a dream come true? More money than most people make in their whole adult lives, just as the kid is starting his. Or is it really a nightmare? The boy's parents were afraid it might be the latter. Their son had lived a very privileged childhood, and was already demonstrating an unfortunate sense of entitlement and a taste for extravagant things. He'd been in trouble at school, and had been butting heads with his parents with increasing frequency. In many respects, their response had been inaction, hoping the situation would eventually resolve itself.

Knowing there was trouble already brewing, think about that boy with an unexpected windfall of $30 million burning a hole in his pocket. I don't know about you, but my mind goes first to the almost certain waste that will follow—money that could be a force for good in one life or, in many, destined to be thrown away on an 18-year-old's toys and hangers-on with their hands out. My mind also goes to a darker side of sudden wealth—one I saw far too often in my years as a financial consultant—parents who worry themselves sick but have no control, broken family relationships, educational failures, flirtations with substance abuse. Trouble, and then some.

Henry Ford once said, "Money doesn't change men, it merely unmasks them." Research suggests he was probably right. If so, it stands to reason that if a man is only 18, if he's spoiled, maybe angry, disrespectful, wasteful, immature—all things that he could grow out of or be led out of in time with his family's support and guidance—if that man comes into sudden wealth, then he's unmasked at the worst possible moment. Where does he go from there?

This boy's parents were so terrified of what their son might do with his inheritance, they hadn't even told him about it. They were dealing with this imminent and potentially life-changing event by ignoring it, just waiting for the bomb to drop.

Now I'd like to tell you about another teenager. Her name is Colette Ankenman. She's about the same age as the young man who was about to receive his trust. They're both from the same part of the country, both raised in families of privilege, and both educated at elite and outstanding private schools. Colette's family is vibrant and active, approaching life with faith, altruism, and empathy. She and her brother Dan have been brought up to believe that they are intelligent, important and capable—that they can achieve great things through their own efforts and those of the family.

When she was just 15, Colette was sitting in a high school classroom when a teacher told the group about a hospital in Soweto, South Africa. This hospital is one of the largest in the world and serves a very poor population. Because its resources are stretched to the limit, the hospital routinely sends new babies home, just hours after they're born, wrapped in newspaper or plastic. There aren't enough baby blankets to go around.

Colette, having been raised to believe she could tackle any problem, decided she was going to do something about this. She sat down with her family and discussed the possibilities, and then she organized and led a community group that knitted hundreds of receiving blankets and baby caps. After Colette shipped that first batch of supplies to the Soweto hospital, she was hooked. She'd made a difference, and she wanted to do more.

With the support of her family, Colette established her own nonprofit, Baragwanath Blessings, Inc., and soon expanded to help more medical facilities and orphanages in Africa, and then in other parts of the world. As of this writing, Colette's non-profit has distributed more than 10,000 handmade hats and thousands of blankets for babies and children in more than a dozen countries.

Colette's family is as enthusiastic about making a difference in the world as she is, and so when the foundation turned its attention to a deprived rural area of Guatemala, they all got involved. The whole family, led by Colette's mom, Jerrilyn, who's a doctor, went on a 10-day medical mission, delivering medications, vitamins, baby formula, and vitally needed care. Dad Gregg, an attorney by trade, served as her medical assistant.

The spirit in this family is infectious. Their cooperation, their willingness to hash out any issue and find a way to the best possible outcome, their generosity, and their affection—you might say they're firing on all cylinders.

Is this family happy? Are they living a fulfilled life? Are they thriving?

Absolutely.

Every family is different, and Colette's represents just one of the countless possibilities—the ways to create a thriving family experience.

I don't know about you, but I can't help but wonder what might have been if the boy whose father was so terrified about his $30 million inheritance had experienced his family with a shared and empowering purpose, with a policy of open communication, with a commitment to cooperation, and with a healthy respect for the good money can do.

It's not a wildly unrealistic scenario. It's a place of possibility. What if that boy's family had been preparing him for a year, or two years, or for his whole life to be able to accept that trust fund and the blessings and responsibilities that came with it? Would his parents still have been living in fear of that event? Or would they have been able to be comfortable, even joyful, about it?

WHAT MAKES A THRIVING FAMILY?

Any family can be a thriving family. Any family can find a way to that place of possibility where each person and the whole entity are cooperative, supportive, effective, and—on good days—happy. How does a family get to this state? Research and experience both tell us that to have true joy, to thrive, a person has to experience fulfillment. Study after study, including those of noted happiness researcher and author Dr. Sonja Lyumbomirsky, find the pursuit of meaningful life goals is a key factor in fulfillment.

And for a whole family to thrive, that fulfillment has to be shared by every member alike.

Fulfillment is such a tricky thing. It's not the same as happiness, because lots of things can make us happy—hearing a baby laugh, walking your dog on a sunny day, solving the crossword puzzle in the *Times*—but those are fleeting moments, not states of being. Fulfillment, though, is deep down. It transcends the passing moments of happiness and sorrow. It's part of who you are. And fulfillment comes from making a significant difference in areas of your life that you care deeply about.

Those areas can be anything—making sure babies aren't sent home from the hospital without blankets; creating something beautiful to hear or see or read through the arts; achieving a meaningful and rewarding career; cultivating a family that loves and supports one another.

Thriving families are all about making these kinds of fulfilling impacts in the world—and those impacts come in all shapes and sizes. So if your family goes to a foreign country delivering desperately needed aid and compassion, that fosters fulfillment. And if your family works together to plan and host a joyful family reunion, that fosters fulfillment. If your family works together toward a shared goal, maybe a business venture, and accomplishes it, that fosters fulfillment.

Thriving families are also made up of thriving individuals. Part of what defines a successful family is acceptance of the notion that every individual in the family needs and deserves to live a fulfilling life—and it's the family's responsibility not just to accept all the varied desires, talents, and paths to self-actualization of each family member, but also to actively help everybody get there. To be clear, helping does not just mean bankrolling a cushy life—that's not a path to fulfillment. But it does mean that if you, your son or daughter, or another family member needs an assist to get where they're trying to go, whether that assist comes in the form of mentoring, education, support, or something else, then the family should absolutely make sure that happens. When we do this, everyone involved sees the family as the place they can always turn to for love and support. This interdependence is a key part of what makes strong and resilient families that can stay together for generations.

Lest you have any doubts as you read this, let me assure you that *any* family can thrive. Sometimes we look at families with challenges—with divorces or substance abuse issues or painful histories of hurting each other—and it may seem too impossible a goal to create unity and find a shared purpose. But that's just not true. Thriving families come in all shapes and sizes, with all sorts of relatives added into or taken out of the traditional image of dad, mom, and kids. *Every* family has a place of possibility worth striving to reach.

WHERE DO WE BEGIN?

Is your family thriving? Think back to your answers to the Picture the Possibilities exercise in Chapter 1. Is your family on track for the kind of future you imagine for them? If not, how do you close the gap between where you are and where you want to be? I've spent the last decade working with families and respected colleagues in my field to create a methodology that fosters a thriving experience in families. In the coming chapters, I'd like to share elements of this methodology with you.

If you're not sure if this experience is for you, take a minute to review the statements below to see if they fit you and your family. If you recognize yourself in them, then the coming chapters may be able to help you achieve your own family's place of possibility.

- *I am a parent who is very concerned about the impact inherited wealth will have on my children.*

- *I am a founder of a self-made family whose financial and business successes have become barriers to having more loving and satisfying relationships with each other.*

- *My family has unresolved disagreements that hinder our ability to feel closer to each other.*

- *I am a young person or adult child who is struggling in the shadows of very successful parents.*

- *My children are exhibiting signs of entitlement and lack of motivation. I'm worried they may fail to launch.*

- *I find myself craving financial management that seamlessly integrates with my family's vision, mission and purpose.*

- *I wish all my advisors were collaborating together on my family's behalf.*

FINDING SOMEONE YOU CAN TRUST

Anyone can do the exercises in the coming chapters at home with their own family, and I encourage you to do so if you'd like. In my role as a family wealth transfer coach, I also work directly with families to guide and facilitate a thriving family experience. The question of whether or not you need an advisor to guide you is a personal one, but here are a few guidelines to consider as you decide:

Is there trouble brewing?

If your family already has issues around cooperation, communication, trust, or wealth transfer planning, the presence of neutral third-party professionals can be a big help in teaching you how to resolve any kind of dispute and in negotiating delicate topics or troubled waters. There are times when a parent or older sibling tries to do this and is perceived as imposing undue authority on other family members.

What's at stake?

When a large inheritance is on the line, the family has more at stake and might consider it a smart investment to hire a facilitator to help solve existing problems and foster cohesiveness in the family. If you are dealing with complex assets, if you've got issues or some damage done already, then you may need a professional advisory team to walk you through the process. Think of it like the difference between using Turbo Tax to do your returns and hiring a CPA—if you've got a lot to lose, it's worth the investment to enlist a pro.

If you do decide to hire a facilitator, there are a number of professional backgrounds that lend themselves to this kind of work. Your ideal facilitator might be a family coach, a trusted mentor, a psychologist or family counselor, a conflict resolution specialist, or some combination of these. Your advisor might have a background in finance or in law, as well. There's no one professional history that defines a person who will do a good job in this role, but there are personal qualities that matter. For example, does your facilitator seem to have the family's best interest in mind? Does the facilitator have the ability to teach your family how to speak respectfully, listen effectively, resolve current disputes and prevent future ones from developing? Is the facilitator cooperative and positive about interacting with other family advisors? Does the facilitator cooperate when someone else has a good idea? Does the facilitator treat your family members and consultants with courtesy and respect? Does each family member feel equally supported and backed up by the facilitator? This is a role that demands neutrality to be effective. As you go through the process of creating a thriving family, you want to eventually involve your existing advisors from other areas—specifically legal, tax, financial planning, investment and/or insurance—and you want to be sure your facilitator is a team player who will welcome that input.

As with anyone you'd consider hiring to do contract work, always check a facilitator's references. This is a person you're going to allow in close proximity with your family and so should be absolutely trustworthy. A good facilitator won't have any trouble providing excellent references, as the work we do has a powerful positive effect on families.

OUTCOMES FOR FAMILIES

As you read and experience the steps to a thriving family in the coming chapters, you'll be experiencing some of the milestones below on your journey. I've witnessed remarkable, wonderful changes in the families I work with in our programs, and I wish you tremendous success in this endeavor as well.

- *Each family member knows, honors, and develops personal talents and resources, and understands how these resources are key contributors to the family's success.*

- *The family recognizes communication dynamics, identifies unhealthy patterns or blind spots, and creates change where needed.*

- *The family develops and documents a shared vision for bettering both themselves and the causes and populations they care about.*

- *The family's planning (financial, legal, business, estate, philanthropic, etc.) seamlessly integrates with the family's purpose and their active fulfillment of that purpose.*

- *Money is a tool for the family to unleash and use to achieve their greatest potential now and in future generations.*

- *The family is educated and empowered so they can become successful investors in their own right, working toward the goal of long-term optimization of the family's wealth. Investing becomes an enlivening and educational experience for the entire family.*

part two

CREATING A THRIVING
FAMILY EXPERIENCE

CHAPTER 4

Look to the Past: Your Family's Story

Every family has a history, and exploring, recognizing, and celebrating that past is an important part of fostering a thriving family experience.

There's an oft-quoted African proverb, first written by Malian author Amadou Hampaté Bâ, which tells us, "When an old man dies, a library burns." It's a powerful observation—and all too true. The experiences of our parents, grandparents, and ancestors are lost to us when they pass on if we haven't taken the time to discover and document their stories. Unfortunately, many of us don't realize what treasures those family histories might hold until we reach "a certain age" ourselves.

When it comes to legacies, a number of studies have shown that people believe the most important inheritance they will receive from their parents or grandparents are family stories and histories—regardless of whether they will inherit wealth. I believe those histories and stories are a key foundation in building family cohesiveness and reaching that place of possibility where you can feel confident your children are prepared to one day carry on your family's heritage in a spirit of capability, cooperation, and shared purpose.

In this chapter, we're going to look at the power of family stories and how you can use them to bring your family together. We'll also discuss the key role values play in those stories and how you can create a permanent and priceless family history that will serve as a shared cornerstone and rallying point for generations to come.

Each of these steps involves an individual activity for you (and your spouse or partner), and then later a family activity. I encourage you to embrace these thought-provoking exercises and share them with the people you love. Some of them are exercises I facilitate with the families we coach, and I've seen wonderful results when generations come together to participate. Feel free to adjust the steps to fit your needs—the most important thing is appreciating the family, the choices, and the values that got you where you are today—and making that history available to your children and grandchildren.

THE POWER OF SHARED HISTORY

Family stories and the histories they preserve have a remarkable power to bind generations together through their shared connections to the past. I think most of us intuitively recognize that there's a lot of significance in family lore, but research suggests it has the potential to profoundly influence our children and grandchildren for the better. Studies at Emory University found that children and teenagers who know their family's history have higher self-esteem, lower anxiety, fewer behavioral problems, more resilience in hard times, and better relationships with their families than kids who don't. That's a lot of benefit for just knowing things like where your parents went to school, how they met, and the story of your birth—all among the 20 questions researchers asked their subjects to see what they knew about their families' pasts.

Why does your family's history matter so much? In part, it's because being a part of something bigger than ourselves helps give us roots. Some experience it as a spiritual connection with their ancestors. Researchers call it a sense of "intergenerational self." It boils down to understanding that we come from a shared past, and that our families will go on after we're gone. There's a certain comfort in knowing you're part of a timeline—or a family tree—that continues to grow and change.

Family stories also give us a critical platform from which to view the world. Researchers found the family stories that most empower kids are not those of ascension ("Our family came from nothing, and look at us now") or downfall ("We used to be on top of the world, but now we have nothing"), but rather, stories of good times and bad, of ups and downs, of failure and success. Those stories provide a different kind of perspective—the idea that every life has highs and lows, triumphs and tragedies; that we are neither doomed nor destined, but rather empowered to wield some influence through our choices and actions. That viewpoint may be particularly beneficial to individuals who've grown up in the shadows of powerful or wealthy parents.

It all begs the question—do adults benefit from learning their family's stories, too? There's a lot less research in this area, but I can tell you that when I work with families to help them foster a thriving family experience, I see time and again how much children of all ages crave information and connection to their families' pasts.

In my own life, knowing "the rest of the story" of my ancestors has made a huge difference to me, has given me a new sense of understanding and appreciation of family, and has made me proud of my heritage—warts and all. I'd like to tell you a little about my family's story, because it is representative of so many families' histories and the ways they become splintered and forgotten when not given proper care.

Most people don't have to look very far back in their family trees to find a story of wasted inheritance or ancestors torn apart by money woes. In my own family, I grew up knowing I could trace my heritage back to a great-grandfather who emigrated from the Cinque Terre area of Italy to California in 1875. He was a peasant—a fisherman—with very little education or money.

Francisco Del Monte settled in the Bay Area, managed to buy some property, and became a successful businessman. As a child growing up in my working class family, I knew little more than that. We didn't talk much about our family's extended history. My grandfather and my father and all my uncles worked in a steel mill. I grew up expecting to find my place in the world there, too—it was practically the family industry.

But my life took a different path—I went to college and chose a career in finance—and several years ago I started researching the Del Monte family tree to see if there was any more to our story. I discovered an amazing fact: when my great-grandfather emigrated, he didn't come alone. Several of his brothers came with him, and later, their parents came to join them. Even though all the brothers were poor fishermen when they came to America, within 10 years they had bought up a great deal of property in San Francisco. My great-grandfather built two hotels. In 1886, one of the brothers opened a restaurant called Fior d' Italia—a place that, as of this writing, is the longest-running Italian restaurant in the United States.

The brothers were tremendously successful and built their fortunes together.

My own family, I discovered, was a perfect example of the *shirtsleeves to shirtsleeves* proverb. There was nothing left of Francisco's wealth, but even more importantly, there was precious little left in the family lore, either. At some point, my great-grandfather fell out with his brothers, and here I was in the fourth generation, not even aware any of them had existed.

That rift in the family had lasted for more than a century. In 2011, more than 100 of the descendants of my great-grandfather and his brothers got together for a family reunion. Until the planning of that event, none of us was even aware of the other branches of the family—despite the fact that we all lived within 30 miles of each other.

Here's the thing I always wonder about: What if we had known about our Del Monte family history? No matter what happened to the brothers over their lifetimes, these men came to this country with no education, no money, and no language skills—and within just a few short years they had created an empire. But I didn't know about it. My cousins didn't know about it. In a generation with 14 cousins, only a few of us graduated from college. What if someone had captured the stories of these ancestors and passed them on to us? What if we'd grown up being told about these brothers who created a legacy of pioneering, resourcefulness, and entrepreneurship? How many of us who never aspired to more than working in a factory or doing manual labor might have gone in a different direction with their lives?

I think it's a tremendous loss that the descendants of these amazing pioneers never benefited from their wisdom and expertise.

— *Exercise* ———————————————

A NICKEL FOR YOUR THOUGHTS

In 1935, when my father was five years old, my great-grandfather Francisco Del Monte used to sit on the front porch of their house and toss him a nickel for each story he listened to. Francisco would talk about his childhood in Italy, about working as a fisherman as a young man, about coming to California and making his fortune—and about many other things I'll never know because I didn't have the privilege of being there.

I've often imagined what a magical experience it would be to go back in time and hear those stories. I'd collect a whole roll of nickels, and I'd still have questions. How did my great-grandfather go from a poor immigrant who didn't even speak English to an affluent entrepreneur? What was his vision? What grounded him to make good choices? What was San Francisco like for him, more than a century ago when he was working his way from rags to riches?

The stories my father remembered from those times are some of the few my family has retained. I hope to help your family practice the art of storytelling and capture your past for current and future generations with this exercise:

Think of a family story of an event or incident you'd like to preserve for your children and future generations. It might be about one of the following topics, or it might be something else that made an impression on you:

- A turning point or achievement

- A value or cause the family has championed

- A proudest moment for yourself or others

- A funniest moment for yourself or others

- A story about family members looking out for one another, or other family unity

- Something that marked a milestone of growth, change, transition or achievement

Write a short summary of your story. Consider including who was there, what relationships and circumstances made it possible, and what is important about having the story be remembered.

You can also use this exercise to note something you wish you knew more about. Use the questions above to learn about the story and then document it.

Family Activity: Ask other members of your family to each prepare at least one story to share, and then plan a family get-together to tell them to each other. If you want to pull out all the stops, a campfire would make a fitting event, but any kind of gathering will work. Pass around a roll of nickels. Each family member should take as many nickels as they have stories to share. Place a bowl or basket in the middle of the group. Go around in a circle and have each person share one story at a turn. Place a nickel in the bowl for every story told. To preserve these stories for the family, consider making an audio or video recording of the event. You can also document the stories and engage younger family members by having them plot a timeline on paper, creating a horizontal continuum starting with the year of the first story and carrying on through the last. Leave room to add more stories at a later date!

YOUR FAMILY'S VALUES

What are the values that helped determine the fates of your ancestors? What are the values that helped you (or hindered you) to get where you are today? A person's values are inextricably tangled up with his or her history and relationships. As you think about and share your family story, consider what values are most important to you. Weave them into the history you create. You can do so by including notes like, "What mattered most to me was that I be _____," or "I believe in _____, so I _____," or "I knew I had to worry about my _____ first." In doing so, you will help your family understand the *why* behind important moments in your life.

Interlacing your values with your history is a great way to share them with family. In my experience working with families, the older generation's values often have a profound influence on those of the younger—sometimes leading them to choose the same, and sometimes pushing them to choose differently. One of the biggest problems I see, though, is when a member of one generation tries to impose his or her values on another. That's just not how the transfer of values works. For example, the patriarch of a family might inform his heirs, "We are a conservative family. All of you will be conservative." There are few approaches you can take in trying to share your values with your kids that will drive them away faster than directly telling them what they must care about and prioritize. And why *would* that work? Every child is different—so different, in fact, that researchers have found siblings are not much more alike in terms of personality than are randomly selected children who aren't family members. Things like birth order, individual aptitudes, and what's going on in the parents' lives at any given point in time profoundly influence each child's development experience—hence the expression, "Every child grows up in a different family."

Rather than tell your heirs what they are or will be, storytelling lets you share your values in a way that allows them to be considered—and potentially embraced. It's a way of saying, "These are the things I've tried to live by, and they have helped me. I hope you'll find them useful in your own lives."

There is no right or wrong when it comes to values. They are deeply personal, influenced by each person's upbringing, education, life experience, and environment. As you reflect on what matters most to you in the next exercise, remember that just as you hope your kids may adopt your values as their own, they may wish you would give more credence to theirs.

—— *Exercise* ——

THE CORE FOUR

Core values are essential, universal, and personal—these are the criteria that separate them from other important values.

Your core values are essential because they are fundamental to a meaningful life for you. They are universal in the sense that they apply everywhere, all the time. And they are personal because your values choices are based on your life experience. Because of this experience basis, a core value may mean something quite different to you than it does to someone else who also prizes it.

In order to share your values and their place in your life story, it helps to thoughtfully identify those that matter most to you. It sounds simple, but most people really need to invest some time and thought when it comes to narrowing down a host of things that are important to just a few core principles.

Below, you'll find a list of 60 core value possibilities. Go through the list and circle or write down the 10 that matter most to you. If one of your core values isn't on this list, feel free to add it. Next, pare that list down to just four terms. If you find this difficult, consider these questions about important moments in your life:

- What made a life-changing experience important to you?

- What lessons did you learn as a result of your greatest trials?

- How have your greatest hardships and successes impacted your life for the long term?

In addition, you can try considering tough-to-prioritize values in pairs—which is more important to you? In the end, you'll have a short list of the values that are essential, universal, and personal in your life—your Core Four.

Acceptance	Accountability	Achievement
Adventure	Altruism	Ambition
Attractiveness	Authenticity	Beauty
Belonging	Charity	Challenge
Collaboration	Commitment	Communication
Community	Compassion	Competence
Conformity	Cooperation	Conservation
Consistency	Courage	Creativity
Curiosity	Dignity	Empathy
Excellence	Excitement	Equality
Fairness	Faith	Family
Forgiveness	Friendship	Freedom
Generosity	Gratitude	Growth
Happiness	Health	Helping
Honesty	Hope	Humility
Humor	Independence	Inner Harmony
Innovation	Inspiration	Integrity
Intelligence	Kindness	Leadership
Learning	Love	Loyalty
Moderation	Open Mindedness	Optimism
Peace	Perseverance	Personal Growth
Philanthropy	Play	Power
Prosperity	Recognition	Relaxation
Resourcefulness	Respect	Responsibility
Security	Self Knowledge	Self Respect
Service	Social Responsibility	Spirituality
Stability	Strength	Success
Supportiveness	Sustainability	Teamwork
Tradition	Trust	Vision
Wealth	Winning	Wisdom
Work Life Balance		

Once you've chosen your Core Four, take a few moments to jot down two statements for each of them. The first should be your definition of the value. (For example: "For me, living with empathy as a core value means always trying to understand where other people are coming from—why they act the way they do." The second statement should explain why this a core value for you. For example: "When I was growing up, my mother always had empathy for everyone—even for people who were unkind. She'd say that someone who was rude might be having a crisis at home, or that someone who was unkind had been treated badly and needed a little understanding. To this day, I can almost hear her telling me to try to understand, and so I do."

Family Activity: Ask your spouse and children to complete this exercise, too. Compare your lists to see which core values you have in common, and which are different. Make a list of shared family values—it can be longer if needed—for use in Chapter 6.

YOUR FAMILY'S STORY

What is your family's history? Do your children know it? Will your grandchildren and great-grandchildren know? How can you ensure that it gets passed on?

It's an all-too-common fact in all kinds of families that the kids don't understand or appreciate the sacrifices their parents and grandparents made to make life good for them. In wealthy families, where many parents admittedly avoid conversations about money, this lack of comprehension can become a serious inheritance issue. One of the best tools you have available to you as a parent to combat this problem is giving your kids a glimpse into how the family's resources were acquired, how they've been protected, and how it all fits into the larger chronicle of past and future generations.

It is at about the time when I suggest documenting their life stories that many of my clients disengage a bit and tell me they haven't got much to tell, or that their kids won't be interested. I understand all of that and respect the fact that not everyone wants to sit in the spotlight—but I strongly encourage you to think ahead 20, 40, or 80 years to future generations of your family. Wouldn't you love to know any tiny details about *your* great-grandmother's life—anything at all? Your own descendants will want to know the same things about you. In fact, they will likely revere you. Doing this exercise now will give your children and your children's children the keys to the library of their history. You've already done much of the work through the Nickels exercise and identifying your core values. What remains is to build a family history—in any form that suits you—that will help give your heirs a peek at where you came from, what motivates you, and what you've sacrificed to give them a good life.

In my experience, adult children overwhelmingly crave a greater insight into the stories of their families—the tales they've watched unfold from the sidelines all their lives. They want to know how and why you made your choices, what mistakes you made, and how you achieved your wealth and success in life. I firmly believe that at any age, our children—like the adolescents in the Emory University study—rely on family history and stories to figure out their own place in the world.

In case you think you might not have much to say, I can honestly tell you that in my years of coaching families and helping them document and share their histories, I've never heard one that wasn't interesting and worthwhile to share with future generations. Most of them have been downright fascinating, like the story of a couple who grew up in Nigeria and eventually became tremendously successful before immigrating to California. The father in that family was one of many children and was not going to be schooled past his primary years. Rather than accept his fate, he ran away from home when he was just 12 years old and worked jobs as a houseboy and a gas station attendant—anything he had to do to continue his education. Today, that couple offers scholarships to anyone from that hometown in Nigeria who wants to go to school. They have changed their world.

Or consider the story of the heir to an American apparel company who talked about going along with his parents as a child while they sold their home-sewn goods out of the trunk of their car. His account of his adult life is full of richly told stories of working with his hands—cultivating the land, building his first house, learning everything by touch and trial—and culminating in the founding of his own successful business in a completely different industry from that of his parents.

How valuable would it be to you to have your own great-grandfather's or great-great-grandmother's story, as he or she would tell it to you personally? Most people would give anything for that—and yet many of them don't even know that ancestor's first name.

Novelist George Meredith once wrote, "Memoirs are the back stairs of history." Each of these families has provided its own version of a memoir—in the form of videos or notes or scrap-books or storytelling—that is a true treasure for their heirs and descendants. They have built those back stairs and preserved a piece of the past for future generations.

Think of the record you're creating as a celebration of your family's history—of your roots and victories and tragedies and love stories. Make it personal and it will be powerful. These histories have a way of taking on a life of their own. Imagine being at that family picnic in 60 years and hearing the story you document today being told by your great-grandchildren to their own kids.

In my practice as a family wealth transfer coach, I use a series of interviews with the matriarch and patriarch to draw out each family's history. My team and I document these stories on video and on paper. If the idea of documenting your family history on your own seems overwhelming to you, there are countless options for getting help. You can do something as simple as ordering a family record workbook that will guide you through the process, or you can turn to any one of a host of professionals who special-ize in helping families document their histories. There's a growing industry of personal historians that includes videographers, ghostwriters, genealogy researchers, and people who do all of the above. No matter what method you choose for documenting your family history, consider enlisting one (or all) of your children or grandchildren to help you. You may well find that someone in the younger generation would love to take charge of this project.

What follows are some guidelines to help you document your family's story. If this seems like too big of an undertaking, try creating a very short version first—a couple pages about your early life, a 10-minute video about what your parents or grandparents were like. Many people find that once they get started, they have lots more to say!

How to tell it well:

- *Plan ahead.* As you envision your story, give it a structure. A beginning/middle/end design works well, and so does a simple timeline. Be deliberate, though, in the way you organize your history. If you want to take things one step further and create some symmetry, consider choosing a unifying element for your stories. For example, build each section around a piece of advice your grandfather gave you or around a beloved place or object that has a presence at different important times in your life.

- *Take the high road.* In writing, just as in life, if you have grudges or strained relationships, try not to let them take up too much valuable space. Strive to be honest, but not negative.

- *Let your voice be heard.* As you tell your life story, whether you're writing, recording, or even working with a writer, rely on a conversational tone. Think about the way you'd tell your family story over dinner—that's the voice you want your kids to hear when they learn about your past.

- *Don't skip over the mistakes.* Your family, especially your children, will appreciate learning about things that made you vulnerable and lessons you learned the hard way. I sometimes find that children of highly successful individuals have a real fear of trying anything—they're convinced they won't measure up. Help your kids see that miscalculations and mistakes are part of *every* life. In the coming chapters, we'll talk about specific ways to encourage your heirs to get past this mindset, and sharing your own vulnerability lays the groundwork for those steps.

- *Remember there's beauty in big and small, high and low.* Try to mix stories from everyday life with those of your major milestones to create a rich portrait from your life. Incorporate the family's happiest moments and also its heartbreaks to let your children see that their story, like everyone else's, is full of ups and downs.

- *Give values their due.* Remember to mention your values—both the ones you live by now and perhaps those you've found were not as useful. In doing so, you'll help your heirs appreciate the underlying "why" in the choices you've made and actions you've taken. Values like hard work, perseverance, faith, education—they are the heart of great family stories.

- *Talk about your mentors.* Who was important to you and why? What impact did they have on your life? Help your heirs understand the value of learning from others.

How to Get Started:

It is one thing to talk about creating this wonderful family history, but it's quite another to actually put pen to paper (or hands to keyboard) and make it happen. If you're not sure where to start, you can use these questions as a jumping-off point. They'll help you organize your thoughts. Above all, remember you're not tackling *War and Peace*. Even if you only put together a page or two of good history, you'll be doing a great service for your family.

Consider the questions below to help guide you:

- If you know it, share the story of your family's coming to this country. Tell about any notable ancestors in the family tree.

- Describe what your parents were like when you were young.

- What was a strong family trait in the home you grew up in? What values mattered most? Describe the difference those values have made in your life.

- What was the most important goal that your parent(s) tried to achieve in raising the family?

- What were you like as a child? An old soul? A troublemaker? A joker? Were you happy, thoughtful, solemn, or hyper? What made you that way?

- What kind of routine did you have in your household? Include a few details about your schedule, meals, chores, and other people who were part of your daily life.

- Share a favorite childhood memory or two—perhaps of a favorite toy, a beloved pet, a family vacation, a holiday tradition, or something you loved to do.

- Tell the story of an event in your childhood/adolescence that changed you, for better or worse. How did those experiences affect the course of your life?

- Share a little bit about your education—where you went to school, what it was like there, whether it came easily to you or you worked hard to succeed, what kinds of friends you had.

- When you were a teenager, what did you want to do with your life? How did your family influence that goal? Did you see eye-to-eye with your parents about your future?

- What was the best advice your parents gave you when you were young? Describe the difference that advice has made in your life.

- Share a lesson you learned the hard way. How did that lesson impact your life?

- What was the first job you ever had? What was the worst? What was the most satisfying?

- How did you meet your spouse/partner? Share a little about your story together.

- If you have children, talk a little about how you felt when you were an expectant or new parent.

- Tell the story of a child's birth, or a highlight from when they were small.

- What memory of being a young parent still makes you laugh?

- What is the biggest challenge of raising a child? What is the biggest joy?

- Explain a little bit about your career, your hobbies, or your interests.

- What is your biggest professional accomplishment? Biggest personal accomplishment?

- What advantages has wealth provided in your life? What disadvantages did it create?

- What values have you found to be most important in your life so far and why do they matter?

- What do you wish for your family when you are gone someday?

- What's important to you about ensuring that wish becomes a reality?

—— *Exercise* ——————————————

SAVING YOUR HISTORY

Use one of these tools to document your family history. Consider making multiple copies so your children and grandchildren can each have one. Some of these histories may sit on the shelf for a while, but one day they will be treasures for your family.

- Home- or Professionally-Bound Family Book: You could call your book *Wilson Family History* or *The Grandparent Book* or *Dad Speaks* or *I Think You'll Want to Know One Day*...Write or type your family story and have it duplicated for each family member. Preserve each copy in a spiral binder or have it professionally bound.

- Prepare a Speech: Put together a 20-minute speech about your family history and record it or have it bound.

- Hire a Ghost: Engage the services of an amateur or professional ghostwriter or memoirist to document your family story. Have a self-publishing company print a copy for each family member.

- Videotaped Story: Script it from your responses above and do a practice run before recording. If you have props available, like family heirlooms or treasured photographs, display them in the background. To make an heirloom-quality video, consider hiring a professional to light and film your story. My colleague April Bell has even created an easy-to-use iPhone app called StoryCatcher Pro that you can use to record your family history. It's simple and really works well.

- Videotaped Family Interview: As an alternate to video storytelling on your own, use a family get-together as an opportunity to make your video. Let each of your children, grandchildren, nieces and nephews or other family members ask a question on camera and then respond to them with your stories. Remind family members that questions that begin with "How," "Why," or "What" will garner better responses than questions that can be answered with "yes" or "no"!

- Scrapbook/Photo Album: Gather your favorite family photos and have copies made, then pair each photo with a story from your family history to create a "This Is My Life" scrapbook.

- Family Cookbook or Travelogue: For a unique twist on the scrapbook theme, create a family recipe book or travel memory book and organize your photographs, postcards, recipes, ticket stubs, etc., alongside family stories to create a uniquely personal family record.

ENCOURAGE GIFTS IN KIND

Ideally, a shared history comes from multiple sources and perspectives. You set a wonderful example by documenting your own story, and I encourage you to take this one step further by encouraging all family members to be aware of their own unique stories. If you have elderly parents, grandparents, aunts, uncles, or other relatives, now is the perfect time to ask them to share their stories with you—or better yet, ask them to share them with a member of the youngest generation and let that person report to the whole family.

Remind your children and other younger family members that their own stories are vital to the family collection. People of any age can be the bearers of tradition. Give your children opportunities to spin their own tales, to think about what makes a great family story. Encourage them to do this together, to talk about times when they were the stars of their own stories and how that felt to them. Ask your children to share their histories and observations with you—you may be surprised to find which people and events loom large in their memories.

In my family coaching practice, I sometimes ask the children (of all ages) some of the same questions in the list above. Parents are often genuinely surprised to discover that the experiences and events kids describe as the happiest, most memorable, or most important of their lives so far are not at all what they'd have guessed.

CHAPTER 5

Live in the Present: Bringing Your Family Together Now

Every family has a culture, whether it's one that's been deliberately created or one that's evolved by default—usually the result of a little bit of both. A family's culture encompasses its rules, roles, beliefs—all the intangible quantities that define how people conduct themselves, relate to one another, and get things done.

Much of what makes up your family's culture is directly influenced by the issues we explored in the last chapter. Shared history and values play into the way you parent, communicate, negotiate, and run your household. But many other factors play into family culture, too—the dynamics between each pair or group of family members, the unique talents and limitations of each person, the time and energy you spend on each other, the habits you fall into, and outside influences of every kind.

In this chapter, we'll focus on steps you can take right now and in an ongoing way to bring your family together in meaningful, positive interactions. These interactions are designed to strengthen your family's culture by building mutual appreciation, strong communication, trust, and goodwill. These positive, productive skills and emotions are the keys to creating a thriving family experience, and in the long run, they're equally important in ensuring your heirs are prepared to take on the responsibilities of your legacy.

In the coming pages, we're going to focus on two major family events—a family banquet and a family meeting. These are occasions you can use to start bringing your family closer together and preparing your heirs to cooperate, communicate, and thrive. These events have worked beautifully for my clients' families in the past, and I encourage you to take the suggestions here and customize them to your own family's unique culture and preferences. Have a picnic, take a cruise, rent a mountain cabin— or better yet, choose a venue or event that reflects your unique shared history. Whatever you choose, think of these events as the first of many. Depending on the logistics of your own family, you might make them an annual, semi-annual, or quarterly tradition. Over time, I hope your family banquets and family meetings will become a distinctive part of the culture you share.

IS YOUR FAMILY READY?

No family is perfect. Not even the ones that seem to be. All of us have disagreements and worries, baggage and squeaky wheels— and there's nothing wrong with that. It's all part of the big, messy, beautiful equation that equals family.

Here's the thing, though: As you move forward with this chapter, and in the long run with creating your endless inheritance, it's critical to bring everyone to the table with a positive and forward-looking attitude. A crucial part of helping your family to thrive is helping them accept each other's shortcomings and resolve the conflicts that prevent them from working together in a spirit of cooperation and love.

Yes, that's easier said than done, but I firmly believe it is possible for any family to foster a constructive, affirmative culture, and I've seen many, many families move from feuding to flourishing using these tools.

There's never a bad time to start working on creating better communication and connections in your family, but there *are* times when circumstances dictate that it's too soon to launch an event like the first family banquet or meeting. If you are dealing with unresolved disputes, substance or other abuse issues, or extreme divisions in your family, it is crucial to address those before you move forward. Asking people to pretend that they aren't angry at each other never works. They've got to get past any major issues before they can work constructively together. Our firm has family counselors and a number of other professional consultants who routinely help us resolve big family issues on a one-on-one or small group basis. The good news is that over the past decade we've seen remarkable advances in the effectiveness of short-term counseling methods for traumatic experiences. The days of individuals or families spending years in therapy to overcome their problems is largely a thing of the past. I've seen even parents and children who haven't spoken for decades, who have carried deep-seated fury and bitterness all that time, sit down at the table together and find a way forward after just a few weeks of professional help.

Please don't hesitate to seek help to work through any problems that exist in your own house. Psychological research tells us that every person craves having a good relationship with family, and over the years I've witnessed some near miracles in families where children seemed lost to their parents, and where hopeless-ness hung like a dark shadow over everyone involved.

GROUND RULES FOR GOOD RELATIONSHIPS

As you begin your family's work together, lay out a set of guide-lines for communication between all family members. When my team and I work with families, we're able to bring a little neutral-ity and enforcement into the room. On your own, you're going to have to dig deep and remember to set a good example. Giving everyone involved the communication skills they need will help strengthen their relationships in the present—and down the line, it will help them navigate their way through more complicated and emotional times.

I suggest you ask your family members to adhere to the following rules for interacting with one another. In my practice, my team prints a list of communication ground rules on a poster board and displays them at family meetings so each person can see them, front and center. We recommend following these effective guidelines all the time, but we specifically ask everyone to agree in advance to comply with them during the meeting. You'd be surprised how powerful that simple agreement is. At the end of this chapter, you'll find a list that you, too, can post if you find it helpful. Encourage your family to continue to follow the commu-nication rules with each other outside the meetings as well. Most importantly, set a good example yourself.

Wipe the slate clean.

Rule number one is simple: Family events are not the place to bring up past mistakes or to criticize other people's flaws. Nothing can derail a family meeting faster than dredging up hurt feelings or laying blame. All family members must agree to leave any baggage at the door so the group can focus on positivity and productivity. Any serious grudges or cases of ill will should be dealt with ahead of time by a properly trained professional.

Treat each other as adults.

I saw my mother during the holidays last year and she asked me, "Richard, where is your jacket?" And just like that, I snapped back to being an immature, petulant kid inside, miffed at being told what to do.

"Mom," I answered, a little whiny, "I'm 58 years old. I think I'm capable of deciding whether I need a jacket or not."

I'm not proud of it, but there it is: My mother unthinkingly stepped into the role of the authority figure, and I jumped to play the foolish child who'd rather freeze than admit his mom is right.

It was not an ideal exchange, but it happens all the time between generations. That "I'm the parent; you're the child" conversation trap is entirely too easy to fall into.

Think about the people in your family you want to reach with your legacy. If they really are children, then you'll make adjustments for their immaturity, but if they are adults—even teenagers—decide right now to speak with them as adults with minds of their own. Avoid pushing the buttons that spark defiance or anger or other childish behaviors. A good facilitator can help your family quickly learn and practice these skills, and you'll be amazed at the results this one simple step will create within your family.

Act in good faith.

There's a book I love called *Crucial Conversations* by Kerry Patterson. The author points out that each of us believes we're acting with the best of intentions when we talk with people we disagree with, but many of us believe the other person's motives are malicious—and so we don't give them the same benefit of the doubt that we believe we deserve.

Politics can be a perfect example. Some Republicans think Democrats are Satan incarnate, and some Democrats think "Republican" is a dirty word, but none of that is really true. Most everybody is acting in good faith. We're all trying our best.

How much more could we accomplish—in politics, in business, and, most of all, in our families—if we just gave each other credit for having good intentions?

Conversing in good faith starts with giving each speaker the benefit of the doubt—never presuming to know what's in that person's mind until it's been explained. It also starts with acknowledging that you only know your own mind, so start your sentences with "*I* think," "*I* feel," "*I* believe," "*I* saw," and, "*I* experienced," and let other people speak for themselves.

Believe each person means well and see what happens from there.

It's not about right or wrong.

Trying to be right, or being afraid of being wrong, inhibits a tremendous amount of honest communication and problem solving. The person who's all about being right will employ one or more of the following tactics to accomplish his or her goal:

- declaring he or she is correct,

- declaring the other person is wrong,

- justifying his or her position,

- invalidating the other person's position,

- dominating the other person, or

- avoiding being dominated by physically or emotionally withdrawing.

If you've ever heard or said the words, "You don't know what you're talking about," or "I can't discuss this with you," you know exactly the kind of communication I'm talking about. The fact is, when we are invested in being right, all we do is keep finding ways to circle back and prove our point—a path that often gets us muddled up in divisive, harsh, unkind, or even dishonest arguments.

In order to really hear one another, in order to communicate in a way that doesn't lead to conflict, we need to set the concept of correctness aside altogether. Instead of entering a dialogue with the intention of proving who is right and who is wrong, enter it with the intention of hearing one another and understanding each different point of view. A good facilitator can help your family quickly learn and practice these skills, and you'll be amazed at how conversations and relationships improve when no one is trying to "win" or reacting out of fear he or she will "lose."

Create a pool of information.

Do you find it hard to think of communication without the right and wrong of things at stake? Most of us do. Here's another way to think about a dialogue or even a disagreement. Rather than two parties with two opposing buckets of information standing off against one another, think about all the information that exists about any given topic as a shared body of water. Kerry Patterson calls it a "pool of information."

The way it works is simple: one person is going to talk and thereby put information into that pool, and then the other party is going to talk and add his or her information to the same pool. And then—this is the big step—both speakers are going to look at that pool of information together and see if they can come up with any new solutions. Now they have a shared goal—figuring out what they can use from the pool together.

Listen actively.

Hand in hand with creating a pool of information is choosing to listen actively to the person on the other side of a dialogue. In short, this means that we must focus our attention on the speaker and what that person is saying—not just bide time until it is our turn to talk again. Show you are listening with eye contact, by nodding, by asking questions, and by repeating back the speaker's thoughts in your own words to make sure you've understood. This doesn't mean you have to agree with everything the speaker says— it means you have to hear him or her enough to simply restate what you think you heard. You can preface it with, "So what you're saying is . . ." and if the speaker doesn't feel understood, then he or she has an opportunity to better explain.

Active communication accomplishes a couple of very important goals. First, it cuts down on misunderstandings based on what we *think* the other person is saying versus what is really intended. Second, it shows the speaker in a positive, proactive way that we are genuinely trying to understand and hear him or her. This tends to take any defensiveness out of the conversation and creates an environment of safety and trust—allowing us to focus on really communicating and finding solutions together. When we feel heard and validated, many problems seem to just effortlessly dissolve. If you'd like to learn more about active communication, the book *Just Listen* by Mark Goulston is an excellent resource.

Tell the truth.

I work with a wonderful business coach named Tracy Beckes, who occasionally confronts me with the dreaded question, "So, Richard, what's the microscopic truth?" This concept, created by authors Gay and Kathlyn Hendricks, means sharing your honest internal experience as you perceive it. It's such a simple idea, but if you think about it, I'm sure you can come up with half a dozen examples of people dancing around the truth in your own life in a minute or less. For example, your spouse doesn't want to go to dinner with your business partner and says it's because he or she is not hungry, or does not enjoy Thai food, or is too tired—fill in your own white lie here—but in fact, the only part of those protestations that's true is the "I don't want to go" portion. The truth might be that your business partner intimidates your spouse, or has said something rude that can't be forgotten, or bores him or her to tears. But instead of telling the simple, if unpleasant, truth, the white lies start flying.

I can't tell you how often I see things like this fester into huge family drama. Whenever possible, tell the truth about how you feel and why, and encourage your family members to do the same by not judging them when what they have to say is not exactly what you'd like to hear. Airing small grievances, fears, and worries and having them be well-received is a stepping stone to being able to work through more complex and emotional issues down the line.

Step outside yourself.

I know this all sounds like hard work—and if you're in a family where conflict dominates, it may sound impossible. But effective, considerate communication is a skill anyone can learn and develop—and once it starts, once other people in your family see that you are making this effort and steering things in a positive way, then everyone starts to get on board.

One key thing you can do when things get tough is focus on stepping outside yourself. Imagine a version of yourself who is hovering above a conversation. Take that slightly longer perspective, and that extra distance may even help you make sense of subtle cues everyone else is missing. For example, I recently worked with a family with a son and daughter, both in their early twenties, who were constantly at each other's throats. The sister was always harping on her brother, saying things like, "You never do what you say you're going to do," "You're so unreliable," and even, "I don't know why I even bother to listen to you anymore."

It was a frustrating situation for everyone, and the brother, predictably, got his hackles up and just wanted his sister off his back.

But when this family started talking—and really listening—about what was going on between these two siblings, it didn't take very long to see that the root of all these harsh exchanges that would devolve into weeks of not communicating at all was not this sister's anger at her brother, but her concern for him. She was worried, plain and simple, and trying to push him to a different path. Her method was having the absolute opposite effect of what she intended—she was driving him away from the people who had his best interests at heart—but once they both understood her intentions were honest and loving, they were able to start communicating in a more productive, positive way.

Train yourself to rise above and look for the real and positive meanings underlying what people are saying and doing—or bring in a neutral party with some conflict resolution training to guide you. You'll be amazed at what you can accomplish once everyone in your family is communicating with respect and understanding.

APPRECIATE YOUR ASSETS

One of the primary outcomes of creating a thriving family experience should be that every single individual in a family comes to understand his or her own strength, skills, intelligence, and unique contributions, and how those attributes are critically important to the success of the family. A twin goal of the process is that each family member comes to appreciate the attributes of everyone else.

When we look around at one another, we should see the skills, experiences, and personal qualities each person brings to the family—not each other's shortcomings. Any schmuck can point out other people's inadequacies. Instead, think about the education, talents, abilities and strengths of your family members. In the coming exercises, you're going to acknowledge those.

Keep in mind that this mentality only works if you count *all* family members as assets—not just the ones you are most fond of or with the most easily spotted attributes. For example, I often find that families have a hard time being appreciative when it comes to in-laws.

I worked with one family in which the daughter of a very wealthy couple married a young man she met in college—a man who came from markedly different background than her own. The family looked at the guy as a threat, a hanger-on trying to get his hooks into the family, and they did everything they could to shut him out. It was a perfect example of an in-law being treated like an outlaw. That kind of reception is a heck of a bias to overcome, and a terrible burden to bring into a new marriage. It's also absolutely toxic to any family.

We live in an age when our children marry for love, when families are dynamic and diverse, when it's far too easy for your son or daughter to just walk away if the partner he or she chooses doesn't find acceptance with you. Why not try a little harder to find what an in-law—or any other family member you feel distant from—brings to the family? You don't have to give away the keys to the kingdom—just try to find something to appreciate about them. Where has this person been? What does he or she know? What are his or her gifts?

Try to think about it this way: In order to thrive over multiple generations, a family needs to be dynamic, not static. What better way inject that necessary dynamism than through the addition of new in-laws who bring different traditions, different kinds of thinking, and new ways of doing things? Later in this chapter, you'll have the opportunity to do an exercise that looks closely at the attributes of every family member, and I challenge you to particularly use that exercise to find new ways to reach out to and appreciate the brilliance of the people on the fringes of your family tree.

EXTEND AN INVITATION

When your family seems ready to move forward, it will fall to you, the initiator of events and leader, to invite your children, grandchildren, and other heirs to the first family banquet and family meeting. It is, as the saying goes, your party—and getting everyone to the table is your job. That said, though, it will be up to each person to embrace the idea of working together for the sake of your heritage and creating a shared future. In order to help ensure success, take every opportunity to demonstrate that your interest and commitment are genuine and driven by your love for your family.

If a family member simply will not participate or accept professional help, I suggest you go on without them. Leave the invitation open so he or she can join you later if things change. In the meantime, feel free to share meeting notes and outcomes to avoid them feeling left out or wondering if the family is keeping secrets from them. This generosity on your part will serve to provide a powerful example of how you'd like everyone in your family to behave, plus it fosters trust and communication. Meanwhile, you'll be working on the rest of the family, getting them started learning to communicate effectively and function well with one another. When the resisting party does decide to join in, he or she will find that relationships are working in a new way—and that can create a powerful incentive to adapt and join in the fun.

The best place to start is making every family member feel loved and welcomed, and helping each person feel that the process you are initiating is worthwhile. If you're dealing with complications and holdouts, be patient. A big ship can't turn around on a dime—and neither can something as vastly complicated as an entire multi-generational family. These things take time and effort.

YOUR FIRST FAMILY BANQUET

One of the tools my team uses to help bring families together is a ceremonial meal designed to celebrate the uniqueness and unity of the family. As the hosts of this critical first event, parents need to come to it with a spirit of humility and hope, and family members need to be willing to put their differences behind them. At the outset, you may not have a lot of goodwill from all family members, but by demonstrating that you know you are addressing a group of worthy adults; that you are open and committed to doing what's positive and empowering for the family; and that you acknowledge past mistakes and aspire to move forward in a loving, supportive way, you can win the goodwill you need to make things work.

Your first official family banquet and family meeting will take you into new territory with your family. Few of us are in the habit of getting together with such an important agenda and a group of goals worthy of a business retreat. But the workings of our families *are* important business. I pair these events together in the hopes that they can accomplish two separate but interrelated aims: Bringing the family together to learn about your goals and intentions; and giving them hands-on opportunities to participate and embrace those goals for themselves.

In the coming sections, there are going to be times for the parents or grandparents—the representatives of the first generation in this event—to participate, and times for you to sit quietly and observe. The family banquet—particularly this first family banquet—is your moment to take the reins and share why the occasion is important to you.

In my practice, I ask the parents—or whoever is filling the highest leadership roles in the family—to prepare for two special moments during the banquet. The first of these is an explanation of why you've brought everyone together, and why it is important to you. Think of it as your State of the Family Address.

— *Exercise* ————————————————

STATE OF THE FAMILY ADDRESS

Presidents do it. So do governors and mayors and CEOs. Now it's your turn to give a state address—your update on the state of your family. This speech is an opportunity for you to communicate the truths and feelings you have regarding your family and an ideal time for reflecting on and sharing your hopes and dreams for them. It is not necessary to delve heavily into specific issues of inheritance at this time. The primary goals of these first meetings are communication and cooperation. That said, though, there's no need to avoid these topics. One of the big long-term goals of fostering a thriving family experience is freeing your family of the taboos of talking about money and legacy. Let your family know that you are thinking about the importance of continuity in the family—not just in terms of financial wealth, but in terms of values, history and culture.

Create a "state of the family" address for your banquet. There is no right or wrong way for you to share your comments. The important thing is for you to be real and heartfelt. You might open with the most basic reason for the dinner ("I worry sometimes that you all might not always stay close to one another," or, "Our doctors tell us we're not getting any younger, and so we think about everyone in this room, and whether we've done all we can to show you how much you mean to us") and tell them this is important to you. In the spirit of fostering continued growth and cooperation, topics might include:

- A positive, thankful description of your family.

- Acknowledge recent milestones and accomplishments by family members.

- The importance of open, honest, and candid communication—noting, if it's true, that you've been practicing.

- The growing respect you have for the ever-changing dynamics in the family.

- Your desire for your family to grow together by encouraging and connecting with each other.

- The importance of creating a rational problem-solving process.

- The importance of building trust and integrity.

- Your hopes for your family's future that include solidarity, cooperation, and a shared purpose.

Think about each of these topic questions and take the time to write down your thoughts. Share them with your family at the banquet. At future family meetings, you'll be able to describe what the group has accomplished and learned since you last met.

After the state of the family address, take some time to enjoy a family meal and to connect with one another. Demonstrate your communications skills by listening actively and being attuned to each person's opinions. Remember to treat each person as an adult with a mind of his or her own. At your family meeting, you'll be sharing all the communication tips from this chapter with the group, but this is an opportunity to try them out on your children and grandchildren.

At some point during your meal, the matriarch of the family or another family elder should be prepared to speak. You need to plan ahead for this task. You have a very special job to do: Tell your family how glad you are to have everyone together, and tell them you'd like to say something about each of them. I can tell you from experience that it is a beautiful and memorable occasion to see a mother, grandmother, or elder of a family get up and move around the table, stopping to put her hands on each person's shoulders and say a few words about what she loves, respects, or admires about him or her. If there are young children in the family, you can ask them to stand on their chairs when their turns come to make this more fun for them. I've seen little girls light up like they've been given a tiara and little boys seem to grow inches taller as they hear how and why they are loved in this special way.

This is an emotional exercise, one that often moves whole families to tears, but it is a beautiful opportunity to start connecting in a genuine, guided way. It demonstrates how important these meetings are to the elders and how potentially beneficial for the whole family.

At the close of your family banquet, ask your guests to think about that family reunion you envisioned in Chapter 1. It is 60 years into the future, and everyone gathers together for a picnic. Some of you are gone; some of you are new to the family—wives and husbands and children and grandchildren. Tell your family how you envision that future group spending their day, interacting with one another, and sharing memories together. Then tell them how important it is to you for those future family members to be happy and productive and connected to each other—and how important it is to you for the family members right there in the room to be happy and productive and connected with each other, too. Let them know that's the legacy that means the most to you.

FAMILY MEETING

Your first family meeting should take the better part of a full day. Try to allow for about six hours of productive time, but be sure to schedule breaks and meals so everyone gets a little down time. After an introduction of the purpose of the day and a review of the agenda, review the ground rules for the meeting. Don't forget the rules are printed on a separate page at the end of this chapter if you'd like to post them.

Next, move on to an ice-breaker exercise that will reduce anxiety and put the family in a happy and relaxed mindset. One of my team's favorites is a 30-minute exercise called *Two Truths and a Lie*. The rules are very simple: With the whole family sitting in a circle, take turns having each person share three statements about himself or herself. Two of these statements should be true, and one of them a lie. After each set of statements, family members have a quick discussion and guess which statement is the lie, then the speaker reveals the truth.

You would think that in families, since everyone knows each other well, there would be no surprises, but this exercise always works. It's fun, and gets people in an open-minded and relaxed frame of mind to continue the meeting. There's often plenty of laughter going around, too.

When you've finished the ice-breaker, offer a quick reminder that everyone has agreed to adhere to the communication rules. It's worth noting that one big hope for this process is that once your family members experience how productive these skills can be, they'll carry them home. I sometimes liken the changes I see when people use these techniques with family members to seeing someone take off an old, heavy, ragged coat on a hot day, and then just leave it behind. They abandon all the weight and discomfort of aggressive, accusatory and impatient conversations, and move forward to lighter, more hopeful, more productive ones.

With some important communication practice underway and everyone feeling good, it's time to turn the proceedings to something a little closer to the long-term goal of securing the family's wealth, harmony and fulfillment. When I work with families, I go through a list of questions about family and wealth with the heirs while the parents listen and observe. If it's possible to bring in a neutral party to ask these questions, you may get a more effective response. But if not, you can have your children take a little time to pair off and answer the questions in writing. Each person may have a different answer, so it's fine if a pair comes back with two responses. The goal is to get them thinking about the questions.

Once everyone has answered the questions, have them gather back together and read their answers aloud. This is a very relaxed process, so if someone doesn't answer a particular question or if a conversation springs up around one set of answers, relax and see where things go. Parents should sit back and listen, but contribute very little. This is your kids' time to speak and be heard.

Every time I do this Guided Discovery exercise with a family, parents discover things they didn't know before. They often say things like, "I never knew the kids liked that trip/place/game so much. They never talked about it." This is an opportunity to gain a little understanding of where your heirs are coming from—to stand in their shoes for just a short time. I think you'll appreciate the perspective you gain from the experience.

—— *Exercise* ——————————————

GUIDED DISCOVERY FOR THE RISING GENERATION

If you have a facilitator, have that person read these questions aloud and let the children carry on a conversation about the answers. Make sure each person has the opportunity to be heard on each topic, but respect the wishes of anyone who doesn't want to respond. Have your facilitator politely reinforce the communication rules, or rotate that responsibility among family members so everyone has the opportunity to tune in for infractions.

If you are working on your own, ask your children to answer these questions individually or in pairs on paper, and then take turns reading the questions and responding as a group. Mom and Dad should be flies on the wall—listening but not speaking!

Questions:

- What was a strong family trait in your home when you were growing up?

- What was the most important goal that your parent(s) tried to achieve in raising the family?

- What qualities from your childhood home would you like to emulate in your own home?

- What was the most positive/significant event that occurred in your family?

- What type of relationship (if any) would you like your siblings to have with your children?

- What type of relationship would you like your parent(s) to have with your children?

- What one principle about wealth would you like to teach your children?

- What do you know about the history of the "blood, sweat, and tears" behind your parents' achievements?

- What's important about making sure the family sticks together in the decades to come?

- What advantages does wealth provide?

- What disadvantages does wealth create?

- Growing up, who were you closest to in your family? Why?

- Who did you most admire growing up? What was that person's career? Educational background?

- In this family, who listens to you the most? Describe that relationship.

- Describe how your mother/father spent time with you.

- What is your favorite childhood memory?

- What was your favorite family tradition/holiday? Why was it special to you?

- What makes you the person you are today?

- What is an important lesson about family you want to pass on to your own children?

- Of all of the experiences in your life so far, what gives you the most satisfaction?

- What do you wish to accomplish in your life?

THE STORY OF YOUR STRUGGLE

After this exercise, it's the parents' turn to speak again. Your objective is an important one: Over the next 30 to 45 minutes, share the story of your life's struggles and successes with your family. I suggest you make arrangements to videotape this portion of the meeting, because your family members will want to hear this story again one day.

As you prepare your remarks for this important opportunity, think about the challenges you've faced, the mistakes you've learned from, the unexpected impacts of events and choices that changed your life. How did you suffer? How did you recover?

In affluent families, it's very common for the kids to put their parents on a pedestal—and for the parents to be comfortable with that placement. I'm always amazed at how surprised family members are when the parents choose instead to talk about their hardships and failures and what it took for them to recover from those things. Grown children often have no idea their dad or mom once went bankrupt or was fired from a job; that a parent may have had a fraught relationship with a business partner; that a parent may have struggled with ADHD or dyslexia all his or her life; that their parents may have had to fight tooth and nail for the marriage that looks so effortless to the kids.

The stories you share are up to you, but the vulnerability you show when you open up with your kids about your struggles will fascinate them, and, more importantly, empower them to let go of their own fears of failure in anything they do. In essence, in sharing your own frailties, you're giving them your blessing to be flawed and merely human too.

Make sure your remarks are shared in the spirit of an adult-to-adult conversation. This is not a lecture or a sermon, but an honest heart-to-heart about your life experience.

Use these questions as a starting place for your story, but feel free to tell it in the way you believe best represents your struggle as a context of your success:

- What challenges did you have when you were growing up and when you were just starting out in your own life?

- What roadblocks stood in the way of your academic, professional, or personal success?

- How did you overcome those obstacles?

- What do you feel your personal shortcomings have been in your life?

- How have you overcome or compensated for them?

- What life experiences have made you a better person? Why were those events so important?

- What do you regret in your life?

- What are you most satisfied with in your life?

- What do you know now that you wish you could have learned sooner or in a less painful way?

Tell your story, warts and all, and let your family see the humility of parents who have made mistakes, who have regrets, who have loved and lost—parents whose lives have been built on love, luck, loss, and hard lessons just like the lives your kids are building for themselves.

LUNCH BREAK

After the parents tell the story of their struggle, lunch tends to be a welcome and wonderful opportunity for everyone in the family to relax and have some informal interaction. This time is often filled with questions from the kids about their parents' pasts and about the story they've just told. It's a great opportunity to just connect and be together in the middle of the more structured exercises of the meeting.

Once your family has enjoyed this break, it's time for the parents to take a step back and let other family members interact with each other. The next exercise is designed to pick up where the mother's speech from the night before left off—taking a close look at the diversity of talents and skills in your group.

—— *Exercise* ——————————

FAMILY BALANCE SHEET

If I ask you about the makeup of your family's wealth, what comes to mind? Most families tend to think of wealth in terms of assets with monetary value: the family business, marketable securities, cash, and real estate.

But let me ask you again, with a different emphasis: what is the true wealth of your family? When asked this question, most people start thinking—rightfully so—not of dollars and cents, but of the value of the people and relationships that define a family.

In acknowledgment that the people are the most valuable asset in even the wealthiest family, why not create a Family Balance Sheet to accompany your financial asset balance sheet? If you are working without a facilitator, prepare the blank chart described below ahead of time, but ask another member of your family to run this exercise. Feel free to participate, but let your heirs take the lead.

Step one:

Before your meeting, use a large sheet of paper or poster board to create a chart of all the members of your family. Ideally, this should be big enough to roll out on a table so family members can gather around and write on it. Create a large box or column on your chart labeled with each family member's name. If you'd like, feel free to include members of your extended family as well as friends who are considered family.

You might also want to create a sheet of valuable characteristics that can serve as an example for your family's reference. You can use a simple list like this:

Educational accomplishments

Business skills

Trade skills

Talents

Travel experiences

Interpersonal abilities

Personal interests and affiliations

Possessions and resources

Special interests

Personal qualities

If you use this list, be sure to make clear that these are only suggestions—assets that don't appear on the list are welcome.

Step two:

Post the list of attributes where everyone can see it. Gather your family around a table and lay out the chart. Give each person a different colored marker or colored pencil. Explain that this exercise is about accounting for all of the wonderful and diverse emotional, intellectual, and social "capital" in the family. In order to accomplish that, ask each person to make a positive, useful comment about their own capital and that of each family member by writing in each column or square on the chart. Encourage the group to be thoughtful and consider all different kinds of skills, experience, and accomplishments, including languages spoken, licenses or certificates, artistic talents, accomplishments in parenting, formal and informal education, ability to build or cook or weld or drive a tractor, as well as personal qualities like faith, generosity, warmth, and loyalty.

Allow 20–30 minutes for family members to work their way around the table and contribute a note to each person's column or box.

Step three:

Look at the diversity of skills and strengths in your family. Look at how different you all are. Let your family know how grateful you are to see such a wealth of talents. Now also let them know that you understand there isn't one kind of fulfillment that matches all those unique qualities. What you wish is for each family member to find fulfillment on his or her own terms. Suggest each person ask himself or herself: "What does fulfillment look like for me?"

Follow up: After your family meeting, ask someone to memorialize your balance sheet, perhaps as a spreadsheet or maybe a fun graphic, and make it available to your family members.

As you move forward from this exercise, consider what your family has accomplished: You created a status quo where all members of your group can come together as equals. Whether it's the big time lawyer, the housepainter, the musician, the school teacher, the perpetual student, or the stay-at-home mom, this tool levels the playing field and helps each person understand that he or she is important and valued.

You have one more sizable exercise to do during your meeting, and this one may, at the outset, sound kind of silly. You and your family are going to make collages. Yes, it's a child's activity, but I can tell you from experience with hundreds of families that it is a valuable and meaningful undertaking.

Why would a cut-and-paste project be especially effective? I think part of the answer has to do with the whimsy of the experience. We are often dealing with very powerful, very mature, sometimes intimidating people. It's very easy, for any of us wrapped up in the responsibilities of adulthood, to take ourselves too seriously—and even easier for individuals who run companies and manage employees and make hugely consequential decisions every day. In my experience, the weight of that seriousness can even be the cause of rifts between individual family members— especially between parent and children and between siblings whose rivalries date as far back to childhood.

And so maybe that's why tapping into a part of us that often gets lost in grade school—simple creativity—and setting aside any "I'm an important executive and I don't cut and paste" mentality as we roll up our sleeves feels so darned therapeutic. This exercise shifts your perspective a little bit. It releases you—ever so briefly— from all the annoying buy-ins of adulthood. And I can tell you that many of these family meetings are worth the price of admission for the kids of all ages when they see their power-broker father or mother sitting on the floor and fully participating in this much-appreciated equalizer of an exercise.

—— *Exercise* ——————————

FAMILY COLLAGES

The family collaging exercise is a wonderful group activity. Embrace it, and see what your family creates and shares.

Set out plenty of scissors, glue, colored paper, pens and pencils, and lots of magazines to cut for photos. Ask each individual to create a collage about the family. Put on some background music, and allow a couple hours for this activity. Then get to work on your collage and watch as your family spends the next two hours talking, laughing, and arranging pictures that represent family to them.

When the collages are done, have each family member take a turn to share his or her collage and explain what the components mean. Typically, these are humorous and quite moving, because people usually think of good things, funny things, and endearing things about their family during the project.

More than once, I've had parents announce at the end of this activity that they're going to frame all the collages and display them in the house, because they so amazingly capture the joy and togetherness of the day.

By the end of the collage exercise, you will have created a strong current of goodwill and positive interaction. You may take this opportunity to talk briefly about some of the statistics from Chapters 1 and 2 and about how much you wish for your family to stay strong and unified. Explain that you'd like to establish regularly scheduled family meetings to use as a means of finding your family's place of possibility and of supporting each person and the group.

This is good time to suggest possible topics to explore at future family meetings, including, perhaps, identifying values that the family as a whole shares, co-creating a statement of shared values (also known as a family mission statement), initiating a family project to work on together, selecting and supporting a charitable cause together, creating mentoring opportunities between generations, introducing family advisors, and finding opportunities for fun adventures.

As you offer up these possibilities, also be sure your family knows you are open to their suggestions. Everyone has to buy in for this initiative to be a success!

Ask for volunteers to plan the next family meeting. If you have a big family, you might form a committee, and if you are a small group, you might have a pair of co-chairs take on the task. Be sure to thank them for taking on the responsibility, and help your volunteers set a few parameters—perhaps a time frame everyone can agree on, a budget, and a main objective.

At the end of a short planning discussion, you'll be nearing the end of a long, productive day. Make time for one more exercise that will help you wrap up on a thoughtful, positive note.

— *Exercise* —

PARTING THOUGHTS

Have your facilitator or a family member read the following phrases—it's ok for a parent to facilitate this if needed. Ask each person to complete each phrase in a way that reflects how they feel the idea relates to the family. Suggest they simply answer from the heart with the first thought that comes to mind. It's okay if some answers are duplicated. If one person is unable to finish a particular sentence, offer to skip them and come back.

- The biggest benefit of today was...
- To be successful, our family must...
- Our most important family legacy is...
- Our most important priority as a family is...
- Someone who wants to be influential in our family must...
- When faced with conflict, our family...
- Our family has been bounteously blessed because...
- It's important for our family to remain strong because...
- In order to stay together for generations, our family must...

Document the responses to this exercise by recording them or writing them down.

At the end of this last exercise, take the time to thank your family members for coming, for participating, for opening themselves up to new ways of communicating, and for allowing you to pursue your desire to bring the family together in a purposeful, meaningful way. Keep in mind that one meeting probably won't change your lives, but it's a huge step in the right direction. As you move forward, make it a goal to keep practicing those positive, active communication skills. Model them for your family. When you create this kind of experience, you make it possible for your children and heirs to take that honest, open, non-threatening communication back to their own homes and relationships. Even though there is still much work to do, I firmly believe it's possible to change the future of a whole family just from that.

ONE FAMILY'S TALE

Even though miraculous changes in family dynamics can't be expected from a single meeting, it is possible and it does sometimes happen. I'd like to tell you a little about a family I worked with a year or so ago. The father hesitated for a long time before he decided to have me work as a coach with his family, in part, I think, because he thought they might be beyond my help. I think he was also worried that upsetting the current equilibrium in the family could generate unwelcome consequences. When we finally did plan that first family banquet and meeting, I included all the exercises in this chapter and a few additional short activities.

During that family meeting, we talked with the children about what they would do if they received a substantial inheritance right then. We then altered the perspective by asking them what they'd imagine their *parents* would want them to do with that same inheritance.

The family's youngest daughter was in her 40s, had dealt with a lot of personal troubles, including past drug use, and hadn't held an adult job in years. She was the family member the parents worried most about—afraid an inheritance would only complicate the problems she already had. During our conversation, she talked about how she'd use an inheritance to take a tour of Europe, and to buy a new house by the ocean. When asked how she thought her parents would want her to use that same theoretical bequest, she got very quiet—and then said she thought they'd want her to settle down, take care of her health, and start a career.

Two weeks after the meeting, that daughter came back to her parents and said, "I've been thinking a lot about that meeting, and I want to get my life on track." She had created a budget and laid out a plan to finish her college degree. She wondered if her parents might be willing to pay for her tuition.

The parents were astounded. This woman was well into her 40s and they felt like nothing they had ever done had made an impact on her—regardless of how much money they'd spent. Now, she was ready to turn her life around.

This family made tremendous progress right up until the father passed away later that year. At the funeral, the children told me how grateful they were for the opportunities they'd had to connect and cooperate and appreciate their father's wishes for them to be independent and happy. In just a short time, they were able to reach a place of possibility that had seemed impossible just months before.

They reminded me, once again, that it's never too late for any family to turn things around. You just have to take a deep breath and start.

FAMILY MEETING COMMUNICATION RULES

1. WHAT WE SAY HERE REMAINS IN THE ROOM UNLESS DECIDED OTHERWISE.

2. INDIVIDUAL PERCEPTIONS ARE THE REALITY OF LIFE.

3. KEEP THE WELFARE AND HARMONY OF THE FAMILY UPPERMOST.

4. LISTEN ACTIVELY!

5. MAKE "I" STATEMENTS ABOUT HOW YOU FEEL AND WHAT YOU THINK.

6. LET OTHERS SPEAK FOR THEMSELVES.

7. ONLY ONE FAMILY MEMBER TALKS AT A TIME.

8. KEEP AN OPEN MIND!

9. DON'T BLAME OR ATTACK.

10. STICK TO THE ISSUES.

11. REMEMBER THE 3 "P"S:

- PERMISSION: You are invited and allowed to say what's on your mind.
- PROTECTION: What you say here stays here.
- POTENCY: You will be heard.

CHAPTER 6

Imagine Your Future: Setting Your Family Up for Success

Conducting your first banquet and meeting is an enormous step toward creating a thriving experience for your family. As you move forward, be sure to stick to the plans for future meetings at regular intervals. Your commitment to these events will help encourage family members to stay on board, too. More importantly, your kids will be more likely to stay engaged because they have hands-on roles in the planning, and those roles will become better defined and more comfortable for them as time goes on.

While there are plenty of essential topics to cover in future meetings, there's an equally important agenda that mustn't be forgotten: making time for family fun. As you look to future events, encourage your children to plan family meetings in conjunction with fun, memorable activities everyone can share. Let the group make suggestions and then vote, or better yet, create a Family Fun committee charged with researching and creating budgets for different options the family can participate in together. Either way, by pairing meetings with recreational events, you'll reinforce the togetherness you're working to achieve, create lasting family memories, and increase every person's investment in the event as a whole.

I've seen families do everything from visiting a dude ranch to skydiving, from sailing in the Mediterranean to a trekking through the jungle in Costa Rica. You can incorporate something as simple as a barbecue, a game night, or a hike—or as elaborate as a safari or a tour through a favorite historic city. You may want to find a beloved spot that will become a permanent family meeting "headquarters"—or gather together in a different place each time. Whatever works to foster the joy of spending time together for your unique family, that's the secret ingredient that helps ensure a successful gathering for your group.

There is, of course, also business to attend to, and each family meeting should include discussion of what the focus of the next event will be. With each successive gathering, your children should take more and more ownership of these choices. I recommend setting aside some time during each of your initial meetings to take the following steps to formalize the family's plans, goals, and systems for accomplishing both. In conjunction with those steps, let your family's interests and needs be their guide. You'll find a list of suggestions at the end of this chapter, but any activity that helps bring the family closer to its long term goals of strong communication, mutual support, and mature cooperation will be beneficial for the group.

ORGANIZE FOR THE LONG TERM

To be successful over multiple generations, every family needs some sort of structure for organization and decision making. When Dad and Mom are at the heart of the family—especially when the kids are young—they often *are* the structure. If a family meeting is needed, a parent calls one, just by yelling up the stairs or down the hall. If the family needs to deal with why the garbage isn't getting taken out, or who will be volunteering for the church picnic, or why Timmy's been in a foul mood all week, a parent metes out discipline, organization, counseling, or conflict resolution to the best of his or her ability. Communication often centers around the parents as well—a trend that frequently carries over into adulthood when Mom or Dad becomes the hub of information for everyone in the family.

The parental organizational structure usually works just fine—until the kids start thinking independently, moving out, starting families, and having lives that aren't so easily managed from the "home office." That's when cracks start to emerge—when family members don't connect, don't address their disagreements, or don't learn to work together cooperatively as adults.

Creating a *family council* addresses all those needs by providing a forum for members to gather together and solve problems, by helping them learn how to become the next generation of family leaders, by fostering effective communication, and by beginning to replace the need for parental governance with self-governance. It's critical to note here that in order for a council to take root and work in any family, the generation that will be running it must have buy-in and ownership. To paraphrase a famous line: If they build it, they'll own it.

All kinds of families—but especially families with an abundance of wealth and power—need to find effective ways to transfer their organizational core from any single individual or couple to a more fluid and durable entity. After all, successful families aren't defined in terms of years or decades, but in terms of generations. You need to be able to empower not just the generation that follows you, but the rising generations that will follow them as well.

I work with families all the time who can't imagine the need for a family council. Some think it's too formal. Many times there are just a few of us in the room—a father and/or a mother and maybe two, three, or four kids. They may call, text, e-mail, and see each other all the time. Why would they need to organize their small band of siblings?

Here's one important thing about families, though: Unless they are making an organized and concerted effort to stay connected, they are forever getting bigger, expanding away from each other, and drifting apart. I wouldn't have to look any further than my own grandparents to see it happening in my family— how far would you have to look in yours?

As families grow in size, their relationships become increasingly complex and chaotic to manage. Your family may start out small, but before you know it there will be so many new relationships to cope with, including in-laws, aunts, uncles, cousins, grandparents and grandchildren, not to mention co-trustees, beneficiaries, co-owners of a family business, or members of a board of directors.

Rather than choosing the status quo—the assumption that families naturally grow apart, gain in complexity, and thereby fail—you can create an organizing entity today that ensures easy and regular contact and support for each family member; a group that preserves and shares family history over decades and even centuries if you're lucky; a team that is prepared to embrace each new generation and bring them into the fold.

Consider this example: In the mid-1800s, two brothers and a cousin invested their combined savings to start a lumber company in Minnesota. They named their company Laird Norton. In the spirit of that very first partnership between three family members, the founders of the company and their descendants have maintained a family council to help keep relatives connected, involved, and invested in the family, and its business, ever since. One top priority for Laird Norton leadership is reaching out to each new generation: teaching the kids about their family history, making sure they have opportunities to spend time with their cousins every year, getting to know them and recognizing their talents and abilities—and ultimately supporting them in finding fulfillment in their adult lives. In fact, decades ago, the stepson of one member told family leadership when he was just 15 years old that he'd one day like to be governor. With the support of family mentors but under his own steam, Booth Gardner eventually served two terms as a roundly respected governor of Washington State. It's a pretty impressive family support system that gets behind a kid with such a big dream and helps to make it happen.

Today, the Laird Norton family extends to more than 400 people and is in its seventh generation. And they are not alone. Successful families all over the world recognize the importance of creating some kind of governance. They might call it a council, a committee, a board, a summit, a team, or something that implies even less authority—depending on the family's unique culture and spirit—but they take the leadership and cohesiveness of the family very seriously all the same.

Often, parents don't feel ready to hand over the reins for any kind of leadership to their kids, at any age. And the issue gets more complicated when a family business is involved. It's understandable—and fine—to want to keep control, but if you want your family to one day be able to manage well without you, the kids need opportunities to experience ownership, leadership, and teamwork.

There's a simple solution to this problem of unprepared heirs waiting to take a real and meaningful part in family decisions and interactions: compartmentalize a project and give them control. The family council is a perfect place to start.

Depending on the size of your family and how the group feels about governance, a beginning council can be as formal and detailed or simple and basic as you like. The most important thing in the beginning is to put a structure in place that reflects an understanding that there *will be* a need for organization and leadership to keep the family together and that at least a rudimentary form of that is being created now. For example, the descendants of John D. Rockefeller began having regular but rather informal "brothers' meetings" in 1945 in an office at Rockefeller Center to discuss family business. Today, those meetings are large and formalized, hosting Rockefeller descendants twice a year.

If your family is ready to jump in with both feet and initiate a family council, make it an occasion. In my practice, we help families write a charter, witness the signing of it, and memorialize the occasion with an inscribed wooden display box and official gavel (all of which you can order in advance of your meeting). These items go to the first council president and get passed along to each president in the future. It's a wonderful way to mark this step in creating an entity that has the potential to profoundly impact—and with luck, outlive—every person in the room.

The first slate of council officers can be selected by the family as a group, by the parents, or by a secret ballot election. Depending on the size of your family, one of these options might seem the obvious choice, but all of them work well. Keep in mind that one main purpose of the council is to put power in the hands of the rising generation, and so in future transfers of power, they should help decide the process.

If the parents select the initial officers, I remind them that this is first and foremost a training tool, and encourage them to select the least likely child as the first president. This does two things. First, it shakes up the existing hierarchy among the children, which is a good thing. It also sends a clear and powerful message to the chosen child that the parents think highly of him or her—which they undoubtedly do—and that they believe he or she can handle the leadership role. Perhaps surprisingly, more often than not, that child steps up and does a terrific job, resulting in a very positive shift in his or her relationship with the rest of the family. That one simple act of trust can be the start of a sea change in that child's life.

In addition to a president, the council needs a secretary to keep minutes of the meetings and track the actions of the family members as they carry out their duties. Also, a treasurer is needed to manage budgeting and any funds provided to support the council's activities. For example, as the first task of the council will be planning the next family meeting, they may start off by creating a budget to work within to make that happen.

In a large and complex family, the council may also include leaders for committees, like a meeting planning committee, education content committee, philanthropy committee, a family newsletter coordinator, etc.

The development of a functioning team takes time. Research suggests there are at least three phases to team building, and both your council and your family in general as an organization can expect to go through each stage as they develop.

The first stage is a group that is simply a collection of individuals. You've enlisted a president, a secretary, and a treasurer, for example, as well as the complicity of all family members to remain organized and cohesive for generations to come. But at the time of this initiative, these are just separate heirs, with individual goals and responsibilities and their own ways of handling challenges and conflict.

The second phase occurs as the collection of individuals begins to acknowledge their shared purpose and responsibilities. They come to identify with the group and its purpose, to define their roles, and to establish norms of working together.

The last phase, the one that is the goal for your family as an organized entity, is the ability to function as a team. As a team, the group shares responsibilities and rewards, works cohesively toward a common purpose, and is focused and effective in bringing ideas to action.

Just like all good things, part of what it takes to develop an effective team from a collection of individuals is plain old time. One day in the not too distant future, it is going to be deeply important for the long-term well-being of your family that this group of individual people be able to communicate, cooperate, and remember that they are on the same side—the same team.

With that in mind, the sooner the process of becoming a functioning team starts, the better.

UNIFY YOUR VISION AND MISSION

To succeed for generations, a family needs a shared purpose that addresses how the family will protect and promote its own well-being, as well as that of the causes and concerns they care most about. It's up to the parents to initiate a conversation about these important issues by sharing their vision—what has mattered most to them and worked for them in creating a successful life, and what their aspirations are for the family. The baton is then passed to the rising generation to create a mission they are ready to embrace for the long haul—a determination of what is most important to their generation, what they're going to do to fulfill their values, reach their potential as a family, and honor their commitments to the causes and concerns close to their hearts.

Parents have a wealth of experience and knowledge to convey to a family's rising generations, but finding a way to share that information so that it will be heard and considered isn't always easy. By working on effective communication and sympathetic listening skills, initiating meaningful family gatherings, and sharing your fears and aspirations for the future with your family, you put yourself and your heirs on a new path. In order to continue on that path, the next step is an articulation of where the family goes from here.

The parents' can move the process forward by creating a Family Vision Statement, a document that represents your feelings, priorities and vision for the family in a way that will allow the younger generations to understand, appreciate, and memorialize them. Regardless of the choices your heirs make now and in future generations, your Family Vision Statement will become an important piece of your family's forward-thinking plan and of its recorded history.

── *Exercise* ──

WRITE YOUR FAMILY VISION STATEMENT

After revisiting your family's history and hosting your first banquet and meeting, I hope you'll find that much of the work of articulating your vision for your family is already done.

Create a Vision Statement for your family. This document can take any format you prefer, but the key components families find most useful are listed below, each with a short description that may be useful as a writing guide:

Purpose:

This section explains that the document's purpose is to convey your feelings and priorities in a format your heirs may choose to use for future guidance. You realize other members of the family may not share the same opinions, priorities, and values you hold, but you nevertheless hope to provide a useful and personal touchstone for future generations. This section also gives parents a chance to convey intentions through a personal statement. For example: We hope this document goes beyond the legal constructs and official paperwork of our estate plan to reflect our deep love and respect for our children and our hopes for a joyful and prosperous future for the entire family.

You may find key elements for this section in your State of the Family address from Chapter 5.

History:

In this section, share a brief history of important events and motivations in your lives. Include some thoughtful comments about your roles as child, spouse, and parent, as well as what family has come to mean to you as you mature and grow.

It will be helpful to rely on the personal history you created in Chapter 4 and your Story of Struggle in Chapter 5.

Priorities:

In this section, list the values that are most important to you and explain why. You may also state why you hope the family might also consider adopting these values. For example: Hard Work: We both grew up with parents who modeled a strong work ethic. In turn, we have always worked diligently in our own lives and careers to succeed. In our experience, nothing that is worthwhile comes without hard work. We hope that a strong work ethic will always exist in our family.

Refer to the values exercise you did in Chapter 4 for the basis of this section.

Financial Objectives:

In this section, list your priorities for your wealth. In doing so, you may impact future family and personal decisions about investment, spending, and other financial choices. For example: Our first objective is our own continued independence and security. Our second objective is the independence and security of our children. Our third objective is ensuring funds for education are available to our children and future generations of our family. Our fourth objective is the continued support of two philanthropic endeavors: our family's scholarship program and providing relief to the homeless of our city.

Family Management System:

In this section, describe the leadership structure in the family (as decided in the previous exercise) and the primary functions of that structure. Those functions might include family meeting planning, dispute resolution, selection of charitable projects, and supporting the needs of each family member. The section may spell out suggestions or the agreed-upon guidelines for participation in family leadership, the projected frequency of meetings, and the hope that the structure will remain strong for many generations.

Refer to your prior family discussions about leadership for guidance for this section. Remember to respect the independence of this entity separate from your authority as a parent.

Vision:

In this section, share your personal message, reflecting on your gratitude for the blessings in your lives and conveying your hopes for the rising generations' well-being. This is your opportunity to share your wishes for your children.

Prepare your Vision Statement before your next family meeting. It can take any form you like—a simple printed document, a bound coffee-table book, or even a more artistic presentation that includes a work of art, old family photographs, or poetry. Present it to your heirs during the meeting. Make sure to offer it in a spirit of sharing—not commanding. Prepare a copy for each family member to keep.

With the parents' vision eloquently documented and memorialized, the next step is for the whole family to agree on a *mission statement* that accurately reflects the group's identity, priorities, and goals. Encourage your children to take leadership in this process. They are the family members who will carry the mission statement forward in the long run, and they must feel ownership of it to fully engage.

A mission statement doesn't have to be long or complicated, but it does need to reflect the shared intention for how the family will work together to benefit its own members and the causes and concerns that matter to them. It's important that every family member have buy-in of this mission statement, as it will be a guiding force in the way family decisions are made in the future.

The essential components of a mission statement are as follows, though your family might elect to include more or fewer to suit your preferences:

- Understanding of the family's purpose
- The family's shared values
- The family's shared vision
- The family's governance
- Inclusiveness and support in the family

- How the family will support the causes and charities they care about

How do you articulate these broad concepts in a way that will reflect your family's personal commitment and deeply held beliefs? You can make a great start by breaking down each of these components and working as a group to define a shared statement. For example, when you consider family values, look back at the values exercise you did in Chapter 4. Did your family members also do this exercise? If not, now is the time for the group to create a list that represents the family. Post the core values of everyone in the group on a poster board. You can kick off the narrowing-down process by having each person put a checkmark next to each value they believe represents the family. Some choices may rise to the top based on how much support they get. Have an open and considerate dialogue about which values should be included in your mission statement. Encourage your newly elected council president to moderate this exchange. If the family is in disagreement, lean toward being inclusive rather than exclusive. No family ever suffered for having too many positive values. Try to narrow your list to a handful of values that all family members can agree on.

You can work through a similar process for the vision and purpose components of your mission statement. Your mission statement can include some detail of your family council and its policies, or simply refer to the council as the organizing body of the family. Lastly, define the way the family relates to one another—this could be in terms of communication, acceptance, support for each person's goals, and perhaps even welcoming of new family members.

It may take some time to work through all the different opinions in your family, but your mission statement can be a work in progress for as long as you need. Have a family member with an affinity for writing draft a version for the group to consider, and revise from there.

Here's an example of a mission statement that closely follows the list of components above:

We are a family defined by our love and faith.

We believe in keeping kindness and generosity at the forefront of our interactions with one another and with the world.

We are committed to being a force for good in our communities and we intend to support one another in our efforts to help others.

We understand that every individual is blessed with unique gifts and talents, and we honor those singularities in our family and encourage each member to pursue life choices that will lead to long-term independence, self-support, and fulfillment.

Here is another example, a short, direct statement devised by a different family:

We are committed to family bonding, community outreach, and fun.

We grow the family assets and provide for the family's education, growth, and security.

The authors of this mission statement go on to define "education" and how, specifically, the family will support its attainment for each member.

Here's one more, a longer sample, to consider:

We are a family committed to our members and descendants continuing a tradition of meaningful interaction, mutual support, and work toward common goals. To these ends, we resolve to:

- *Preserve our annual tradition of gathering together to celebrate our ancestry, discuss family business, and enjoy each other's company.*

- *Maintain a family council to provide leadership and organization for our shared endeavors.*

- *Respect and celebrate each family member's unique personality and talents.*

- *Promote a loving, kind, and welcoming atmosphere for existing family members as well as those who become part of our family in the future.*

- *Express our gratitude for our many blessings through support of philanthropic projects.*

- *Communicate with one another in a spirit of honesty, kindness, and mutual respect.*

As you can see, this document can be whatever your family needs it to be. Focus on what everyone cares about and envisions empowering the family for the long run, and you'll end up with a mission statement that will hold up as a cornerstone for your family's future.

FIND A SHARED PURPOSE

When I first meet with new families, I often recommend a preliminary step while they consider their legacy and the work the family needs to do to reach its place of possibility. I ask them to go home and talk to their kids—regardless of whether the "kids" are in grade school or in their 40s or 50s—and ask what problems they see in their town, in their school, in their church, or in any other area that impacts their lives that the family could work on together to make a difference. Inevitably, this conversation lights a spark. In just that one dialogue, many families come up with a game plan to go out and make a difference. This spirit of service and giving can impact any person at any age, but the sooner it starts happening for your kids, the better it will serve them over the course of their lives.

We've talked in some detail in this book about the potential damage wealth can do to heirs, whether by encouraging an attitude of consumerism, discouraging the motivation to be self-supporting, or enabling and worsening destructive vices. But the flip side of those dark possibilities is opportunities for love and light. Those possibilities are one of the biggest reasons I get up every morning and love the work I do. Helping families communicate, cooperate, and find ways to use their wealth and power to positive ends is deeply fulfilling and gratifying. When I look at families who throw themselves into philanthropic endeavors like making sure smart kids from poor families can go to college, sending supplies to underfunded hospitals and orphanages around the world, and reaching out to underserved populations in their communities with caring and compassion—it gives me great hope for the world my children and yours will inherit one day.

What is the highest and best use of wealth if not employing it for the greater good? If you can show your children that serving other people is one of the greatest opportunities to find joy in their lives—greater by far than the satisfaction that comes from consumption—you will give them a perspective that will enrich them now and always.

People often ask me if philanthropy is one of the keys to creating a thriving family and preserving wealth from generation to generation. I think the most honest answer may be that while it doesn't necessarily have to be a component, almost every family I can think of that has truly achieved their place of possibility is involved in some charitable endeavor together. These endeavors often take traditional forms through charities and philanthropic organizations, but sometimes families choose to create other kinds of service opportunities—like bringing dinners to friends or neighbors who are ill or homebound, or helping with the upkeep of someone's home or property. Volunteering your time and talents in any form helps support and strengthen your thriving family.

Why does it work? There are several key reasons:

- Philanthropy and service give family members a purpose outside themselves. Because of its nature, this purpose calls on each person's compassion, empathy, and sense of personal and shared responsibility—meaning everyone becomes truly engaged and committed. This isn't just my own experience talking—myriad studies done with children and adults of all ages and in every corner of the world bear out what we all know to be true: helping others makes us happy.

- Working toward a shared cause puts all family members on the same team, striving toward a definable goal. Divisions within the family must be set aside or left behind for the group to succeed in its goals.

- Engaging in a long-term philanthropic or service project gives family members excellent practice in communicating and cooperating with one another, as well as in facing logistical challenges and roadblocks and working through them together.

- Charitable work, when done with a personal connection to the cause, is a profound and impactful reminder of the great need that exists in the world and the potential for each individual—and each family—to make a significant and positive difference.

- Philanthropy allows parents and all family members to demonstrate that they are living in a way that's in keeping with their values—something the rising generation will recognize and respect.

To be clear, the charitable component of thriving families is about much more than money. In fact, it can be achieved with equal or better results in your family without spending a dime if you prefer to dedicate time, services, labor, goods—any useful contribution to a cause your family deems worthy can achieve this goal. Two useful websites for finding worthwhile projects in your local community are *www.justserve.org* and *http://www.volunteermatch .org/*.

To foster closeness and cooperation, it's important to engage the whole family in choosing a philanthropic project. Be sure your selection is long term enough to require everyone involved to cooperate and work together. Consider the following exercise to come up with a cause your family can rally around:

—— *Exercise* ——————

CHARITABLE CHALLENGE

Step One: Begin by allocating a dollar amount to your family's philanthropic project. It can be anything—$100, $1,000, $1 million, or $10 million. At your next family meeting, explain that you would like to allocate this portion of your assets to charity. If you wish to formalize the undertaking, speak with a trusted advisor about setting up a specialized account for this purpose.

Step Two: Ask each family member to spend some time researching and considering potential beneficiaries before the next family meeting. Each participant should come to that meeting with three lists. The first list should contain the topics that really have a deep and personal resonance with the participant. The second list should contain topics the participant is eager to work on. The third list should contain topics the participant feels confident can be addressed by the family—accomplishable goals.

At your next family meeting, with the council secretary keeping a shared list on an easel or dry-erase board, ask each person to share his or her selections. As the parents endowing this effort, you may need to determine how many different endeavors the family will undertake, but let your children lead the discussion about the topics and their feasibility. Help the family move toward a consensus, making sure everyone involved feels some ownership of the choice.

Step Three: Engage family members in reaching out to the charitable organizations in question, perhaps visiting them, to evaluate the strength of their mission and their ability to manage a gift wisely. If appropriate, you might ask a professional advisor to review the entities' financials and explain the numbers to the family.

If possible, try to incorporate a personal, hands-on element with your selections. This can be anything from a huge commitment like the family traveling together on a mission trip, to something simpler, like spending an evening providing and serving dinner at a homeless shelter.

Step Four: After your project is complete, follow up with the charity to learn if your contribution was impactful. If it was, share those impacts in your next family newsletter or discuss them at your next meeting. Celebrating successes is not only positive and fun, but will help build a family culture focused on service. Consider making this kind of project an ongoing component of your family's events.

FUTURE FAMILY MEETINGS

The only real limitation on what can be planned for future family meetings is the imaginations of the organizers. Encourage your children to take the lead for these events, coming up with suggestions, nailing down the specifics, and organizing food, lodging, and an agenda. Be available to consult and help, but give them plenty of room to run their own show and demonstrate their capabilities. Here are a few suggestions for successful meeting themes and events:

Assessment Day: Most of us think of personality, communication, leadership, and social style assessments as the tools of corporate HR departments, but the fact is, these assessments can give family members incredibly useful insights into how each person thinks, functions, and interacts with the others. These insights help improve the family's levels of trust and communication. In the safety of a warm family environment, they can also be a fun and fascinating way to spend a day together. One easy and fun personality indicator for the family to use together is called *Kingdomality*. This free online assessment tool puts you into one of several different medieval personality archetypes, such as White Knight or Dreamer Minstrel. Other useful facilitated assessments include Stratton ILS, DISC, Myers Briggs, Kolbe, and ProScan.

Work Together Day: Think of something your family can build together. It can be as elaborate as a tree house or as simple as a special meal to commemorate an important event. One family purchased two dozen children's bicycles and spent the day assembling them before donating the lot to charity. Engage family council members to plan this event in advance and ensure everything the family needs is available; then roll up your sleeves and get to work.

Get Out of Your Comfort Zone Day: Take a ropes course (you can find them at almost any levels of ease or difficulty); go canoeing or kayaking; practice trust exercises in the backyard. Choose an activity that is new and unfamiliar to everyone in the family and take it on as a team, working together to ensure everyone enjoys and learns from the experience. A facilitator would be very helpful for this kind of activity.

Family or Cultural History Day: Give each person a portion of your lineage to research and then combine all that homework to create a giant family tree during your meeting. Some online resources for doing this include familysearch .org and ancestry.com. Alternately, you could enlist an expert or artist with ties to your cultural background to come and share knowledge or talents that pertain to your heritage. You could combine this day with a group outing to a cultural festival or event.

Bring on the Advisors: Invite important family advisors to come and meet with your family. Ask them to explain what service they provide and why it is important to the family's well-being. This event could be tied together with educational training in each advisor's area of expertise, such as workshops on investment skills, tax advising, or estate planning.

part three

ESTATE PLANNING FOR THE THRIVING FAMILY

CHAPTER 7

Preparing the Rising Generation

All the steps and ongoing efforts your family makes to achieve its place of possibility—to become a group who shares past, present, and future in a loving, cooperative way—benefit your children and rising generations long into the future. A family that has figured out how to thrive, how to communicate and cooperate, celebrate, and support each other, is empowered in every aspect of life.

With these great strides toward fostering your family unity underway, it's time to turn your attention to steps you can take to help prepare your heirs to one day be good stewards of your family's wealth, history and traditions.

John D. Rockefeller once wrote, "Giving should be entered into in just the same way as investing. Giving *is* investing." It's a wise piece of advice from a man whose heirs are still today controlling a fortune believed to exceed $10 billion. In the context of family gifts, I believe every hour and day you invest in preparing your heirs to be able to accept and perpetuate your family's legacy is time well spent. This chapter outlines eight steps you can take now to ensure the rising generation of your family will be ready and able to cope with the responsibilities that come with inheriting financial resources.

1. Embrace the Individual.

It's critical for each rising generation to discover for themselves what constitutes a fulfilling life. How can you help your children do something so intensely personal? First, clear the way by letting them know your hopes for the future are for their health and happiness, in whatever form that takes. Encourage them to learn, grow, and develop their own talents. Make sure your children know your own life has been shaped as much by your failures as by your successes, and that you fully support them in going their own ways, following their own passions, and making their own mistakes.

My colleague Jay Hughes and his coauthors write in their book *The Voice of the Rising Generation* about the "black hole" that can be created by highly successful and wealthy parents—an entity that threatens to sap the dreams and aspirations of future generations. The idea that Dad or Mom's success could cost the children their own chance to thrive is a parent's nightmare, but it doesn't have to be that way. For every headline-grabbing child of wealth who flounders and makes terrible choices, there are others who are living quiet and fulfilling lives in which family money is a force for good.

Thoreau once wrote, "Wealth is the ability to fully experience life." Make sure your children have the opportunity to figure out for themselves what that full experience is all about.

2. Encourage Empathy.

If there is one characteristic lacking in every ungrateful and over-indulged kid or spoiled adult you'll ever meet, it's empathy. Here is arguably the single most important relational skill, the one that is the root of understanding, kindness, charity, and respect—and yet it's often grossly underdeveloped. Empathy can be the key to healthy relationships within families and outside of them, and it can, mercifully, be learned at any age. You can demonstrate empathy in your family in the way you interact with each member, by emphasizing that you hear and understand where they're coming from. You can also show it in the ways you relate to and reference everyone from your spouse to your secretary, your church leader, or a stranger on the street.

Empathy is a skill that requires practice, and there's no better place to start than within the safety of the family. At your next family meeting, commit some time to empathy exercises like the paired practice below. The experience can help your children be more considerate of one another and in their interactions in the wider world.

—— *Exercise* ——————————————

PAIRED EMPATHY PRACTICE

We all know the saying, "Charity begins at home." Well, empathy begins at home, too. Practice taking on a different person's point of view is a simple but invaluable tool in teaching your children how to relate to and understand others.

Team up pairs of two family members—sibling pairs are ideal. Have each pair sit down facing one another. Choose one person from each pair to be the speaker and one to be the listener. Ask the speaker to tell a story about a time when he or she felt successful. Allow five minutes to tell the story.

Next, ask the listener to repeat back the story telling both what happened and how the speaker felt. Allow two to three minutes.

Now reverse roles and let the first listener speak and the first speaker repeat. Remember that the repeater must explain both what happened and how the storyteller felt at the time. You can also try this exercise with each speaker sharing a situation where they felt sad, threatened, or hopeless. What makes this exercise powerful is the fact that the listeners know they have to repeat the story back, so they listen actively and really tune in to the facts and emotions of the story. The practice takes on a whole new and deeper dimension when the paired participants are family members. Many times, our greatest failures to effectively communicate occur in these relationships we take for granted.

---

3. Foster Altruism.

Helping your children learn and understand that service to others is the path to some of life's greatest joys is like giving them the keys to the kingdom—it opens up a whole world of positive possibilities. One way to effectively demonstrate this concept is to model it in your own life---showing compassion in your words and actions. If your children spend their lives watching you express humility and gratitude for your wealth through your philanthropic endeavors, they'll be more likely to develop their own sense of responsibility to others.

When you encourage your kids to think about and help others, you're also helping them find contentment in their own lives. There are multitudes of studies on the psychological benefits of giving. As Harvard professor and author of *Happy Money* Michael Norton says, "If you think money can't buy happiness, you're not spending it right." Study after study finds that people who donate their time and money to help others are happier and more satisfied with their lives than those who do not.

Your best course of action—after demonstrating altruism yourself—is in helping the rising generation discover their own values, goals and aspirations for the causes they care about. This exploration is best and most effectively done over time and *before* an individual receives a windfall inheritance—an event that can color perceptions and put undue pressure on an unprepared heir. How much better for your children to find causes that matter enough to them to give their own time and money before they inherit substantial wealth?

If your family does the charitable challenge in Chapter 6 or any other small-scale charitable endeavor and finds it rewarding, consider setting up a donor-advised fund or—if you are ready for a bigger commitment—a private charitable foundation, to continue supporting the family's philanthropic efforts.

4. Teach Effective Communication— About Everything, Including Money.

It's not possible to overestimate the value of teaching your children to communicate honestly and effectively. Their personal and professional relationships will benefit immeasurably for learning the communication techniques we discussed in Chapter 5, and when the time comes for them to inherit, those skills will help them work with one another and with outsiders to effectively steward the family's financial and cultural journey. Another benefit is that when your children are communicating effectively at home, they are modeling those crucial behaviors for their own children.

Make sure your family's effective communication doesn't stop short of broaching the subjects of wealth and inheritance. Too often, parents are terrified to discuss their wealth with their children, largely out of fear that it will provide a disincentive to work. However, by not being open and forthright about the family's circumstances, those same parents are committing a potentially devastating mistake. Withholding this vital truth is the opposite of open and honest communication, and it epitomizes the lack of trust that contributes to failed family fortunes.

If there's one thing I've learned with certainty in my years coaching families about wealth, it's that silence about financial matters is not golden---it is destructive and dangerous. For everyone's sake, talk with your children about money. Don't just say, "We're very blessed," or "We have enough." Talk with your adult children about your wealth—how much there is or will be, what it means to you, what you hope it means to them, and about its power to be a force for good—or for harm—in the world.

Time and time again, I meet heirs who've been completely blindsided by sudden wealth—and who've coped with the shock by withdrawing from family and friends, by spending like there's no tomorrow, by giving it all away, or by charging down paths of self-destruction ironically made possible by their family's financial legacy. The fact is, you can train your children how to deal with an inheritance to come; it's more difficult to reverse the damage caused by the deceit of withholding the family's true story.

Give your heirs time to think about and process the implications of future inherited wealth and help them start to prepare for that eventuality as soon as you possibly can.

5. Demonstrate and Expect Trust and Trustworthiness.

Hand in hand with effective communication in families comes trust. This is an issue for all families and all children, but it's a particularly big issue for families with substantial wealth. In these families, I sometimes see a tendency to close ranks and become insulated and protective. Yet we all have to be able to function not just within our families—but also in the wider world—with some level of trust. You want your kids to have that, and the sense of security that comes with it, long before a financial windfall comes into their lives.

Part of fostering trust in your family is simply in the way you create it—being trustworthy and expecting your children to be trustworthy in return. There are a few simple steps you can take to start building trust with heirs at any age:

- *Be honest.* Your family needs to know not only that you are a person who tells the truth, but that you are also genuine and authentic in the things you say and do. This kind of honesty goes beyond sharing facts to also sharing feelings.

- *Be consistent and reliable.* At any age, children look to parents for constancy. It's a great comfort to a member of the next generation who's just figuring out who he is or what she wants to be to know that Dad or Mom can be counted on to show up, to be encouraging, to react within a predictable range of expectation, to always love you. Years ago, I read an interview with a starlet who said her father had taken her to Paris when she was a young teen because, he told her, "I want your first trip to Paris to be with the one man who is going to love you for the rest of your life." That kind of sentiment of absolute security within the family, with or without the trip to Paris, creates a bedrock of trust your kids can lean on when life gets complicated or rough.

- *Be accountable—even if that means being sorry.* Nobody's perfect. We all make mistakes—but when that happens, we have to take responsibility. A true apology, the kind that can help foster healing, is offered with intellectual and emotional honesty—recognizing both the fault and the damage it has caused—with no expectation of anything in return. It's no easy feat for a parent to go hat-in-hand to apologize to a child, but building trust and peace in your family sometimes means admitting to mistakes and failures so you can move on.

  Rest assured that an apologetic gesture isn't nearly as one-sided as it may feel at the time. Your actions and words, even with your adult children, set the tone for future dialogues to be equally genuine and humble.

- *Be trusting.* Unless you have strong and compelling reasons not to trust in the rising generation in your family, trust your kids enough to let them step out on their own, try on leadership and ownership roles, and learn from their successes and mistakes. It's hard to step back and let events unfold without your influence, but it is the best way to ensure your own fears and insecurities don't hinder your relationships with your kids.

If you feel your kids aren't trustworthy yet, you can start working on building trust between you by giving them stewardship over things that aren't crucial to the family's success, and then letting them work their way toward more important responsibilities as they prove their reliability and good judgment.

6. Teach and Model Impulse Control.

There's an infamous Stanford study from the 1960s that found children who could control the impulse to take a marshmallow for 15 long minutes had better outcomes on a whole slew of measures as they grew and matured. Self-control, it seems, is linked to success in school, in business, in marriage—in almost every area of life. More recent work, including a 30-year New Zealand study, found children with high self-control grew into adults with greater physical and mental health, fewer substance-abuse problems, and better savings behaviors and financial security than those who lacked it. The patterns remained even after researchers made adjustments for socioeconomic status and intelligence.

Now, if you're reading this book, there's a good chance you're long past starting with preschoolers and marshmallows to work on impulse control, but the value of this attribute doesn't diminish when we become adults. As I mentioned in the very beginning of this book, money is like an accelerant—it can ignite your best plans, or your worst vices—and grow them into wildfires.

How can you help foster impulse control in your family's rising generation? For starters, acknowledge your own failings in this area and potentially inherited or learned contributing factors. If a short temper, unhealthy relationships, or a weakness for alcohol have factored into your own impulse issues in the past, talk about it with your family—and share the choices you've made to reduce the potential for trouble. For example, you might talk about exploring whether you have a serious dependency issue or seeing a psychologist to get at the root causes of an anger issue. Show your family that these steps don't come easily to you, but that you work at them.

Another way to help your kids practice impulse control is by giving them opportunities to practice these skills. The *Family Bank* exercise later in this chapter offers one useful way to do so.

7. Teach the Importance of Budgeting.

Every generation and every child needs to learn how to budget, to live within their means, and to know how much money is "enough." Regardless of whether your children are going to inherit enough money to buy a car, a house, or a small city, they need to be able to understand and respect the value of creating a budget and sticking to it. There is no level of wealth that precludes the necessity of being responsible with money. The first step you can take to help ensure your kids learn this skill is one many parents struggle with: Talk about it. A recent University of Arizona study confirmed what financial advisors and family wealth transfer coaches see every day—the fact that students who are responsible with money are those most likely to have parents who talk with them about financial matters and expect them to make good financial decisions.

Another important step is learning the value of hard work. Every person needs a fundamental understanding of how labor over time begets income, and how that income is implemented to meet one's needs. Talk with your kids about wages and salaries, about the hours of work it takes to pay for a car or a house or a college education. Encourage and reward steps toward becoming self-supporting and contributing members of the family and society.

If your kids are young, start them off early with an allowance they have to manage and use for specific expenses. For example, for an elementary school-aged child, allowance money might need to be tapped for toys, gifts for family members, and trips to the movies or other social events. Older children might also be expected to cover the costs of their cell phone plans, of social outings, and of gas for the cars they drive. There's nothing wrong with providing enough allowance to cover these costs, but expecting your children to budget that money and use it responsibly so it is enough to cover their obligations and extras provides a valuable life lesson.

You can also help your children to learn budgeting skills by giving them experience managing limited amounts of money. I often encounter families who give their children the maximum annual tax-free gift ($14,000 at this writing) each year, with no strings—or even suggestions—attached. Some of these same children will one day inherit vast fortunes. Will they know how to manage that money?

Why not give a gift now that's designed to teach a valuable lesson for the long run? You might call it a "trial inheritance." Give that same annual gift to your children, but ask them how they intend to spend it and why—and ask for an accounting of that spending at the end of the year. This is not—and should not be—an exercise in being judgmental or critical. It's an exercise for your heirs in planning how they will use X amount of money—and then in reflecting on how those plans succeed or fail. This is a wonderful and effective way to begin mentoring the rising generation in your family about recognizing and valuing the best uses of money for their individual circumstances.

8. Share Investment Knowledge.

Some time ago, I worked with a family whose father was very ill and concerned about what would happen to the family fortune upon his passing. When the whole group gathered together, I realized how very overdue that concern was. The family has a unique and complicated income structure based on property ownership and leases. The heirs, in their 40s and 50s, not only didn't know how this financial process worked, they didn't even know it existed. The parents had never told them about it, and the children had never asked.

If you want your kids to be successful stewards of your family's fortune, then you have to teach them how to manage money. At the very least, they need a basic understanding of investing, risk tolerance, realistic return expectations, tax liability, the importance of trusted advisors and how to select them, and the potentially misleading nature of the financial press. If your assets include a family business they will one day inherit, they will need to learn the ins and outs of that as well. These are not skills that are learned by receiving an allowance or by holding an entry-level job. They are skills you must go over and above to make sure are part of your children's education.

You can certainly enlist the help of trusted family advisors to teach financial management, but I don't recommend completely outsourcing this job. Part of your critical role as a parent is in the way you show your heirs the links between values and money. This aspect of financial preparation will have a greater impact on your kids if they learn it from you.

Teaching investment and financial basics to your kids has long-term implications on many different levels. They will be better prepared for the nuts and bolts of wealth, better able to appreciate the assets they will inherit, and better able to recognize the intentions of future friends, acquaintances, or even advisors who might seek to manipulate them for their wealth.

9. Teach Family Members to Work Together.

Many siblings, cousins, and other relatives know how to relate to one another perfectly well in their familial roles, but being business partners or co-trustees requires a different kind of relationship. Regardless of their individual abilities and goodwill toward one another, family members need to learn how to work together in the roles they'll hold in the future. Consider this analogy: If you take 22 great football players and have them spend an afternoon hiking or playing cards or having beers together, do you think they'll be prepared to take the field and play a game on Sunday? Of course not! They have to practice together, with each person playing in position, to be ready for the unique challenges of a game.

The analogy applies equally well to family members who will one day be responsible for a family's business, legal, and financial affairs. No number of family picnics and game nights is going to get them ready for that. The question isn't *whether*, but rather *how*, you can prepare the rising generation for those roles. The next exercise, a Family Bank Project, is a great place to start.

—— *Exercise* ——————

FAMILY BANK PROJECT

One especially effective tool for practicing money management is the formation of a "family bank." The long-term purposes of a family bank might include having a shared pool of capital that the family, working together, could use to provide funding for the family's meetings; for providing loans to family members starting a business or buying a house; and for scholarships for members of the extended family. The sky's the limit when it comes to the number of possibilities a family bank could accomplish over time.

To get started with this project, the parent(s) write a single check to all of the kids and tell them, "We want you to manage this money, to invest it and come back to us in a year and show us how you did." The kids tend to think they've got to hit this out of the park—to demonstrate a substantial return on investment— but mom and dad mostly want to see if the family can work together and to give them a chance to learn and make mistakes when there are close limits on the potential damage that can be done. The goals of this project are many, including:

- Making the children stewards of money that cannot be consumed;

- Encouraging the whole family to talk about money together;

- Learning to invest;

- Learning to make cooperative decisions;

- Learning to engage professional advisors; and

- Learning important leadership skills.

Your children should identify and interview different financial advisors to work with. During the interviews, they should learn about the strategies advisors use to manage money, how they are compensated, and how they will communicate with the group. The advisor should, at a minimum, help them understand different types of investments and how each behaves, help them understand investment risk and returns, and help them create an Investment Policy Statement that describes how the funds will be invested. The policy should include:

- Potential future use/purpose of funds;

- Appropriate time horizon for investing the funds;

- Your desired rate of return over the time horizon;

- The appropriate amount of risk you are willing to take to achieve your desired rate of return;

- Level of current income desired;

- Anticipated annual withdrawals; and

- Desired level of liquidity.

Once a policy is established, decide what type of entity is appropriate to own these funds, and open the account. Come to an agreement about signatures required to access it. Make sure your children are the ones who lead and par-

ticipate in all the discussions. After all, the purpose of this exercise is training the heirs! If you as the parent are personally involved, the default way your family operates will just continue, and so not much will be learned. Invest the money and establish regular family bank meeting dates (quarterly is ideal) to review and discuss the progress of the family bank portfolio.

Don't put your focus on the performance of the funds. Wouldn't it be better for your children to make mistakes and do their learning in this situation, where the stakes and potential losses are minimal, than for them to make them later when they inherit all of your wealth?

All of the issues the family bank addresses are the kinds of things the rising generation is going to have to deal with one day when mom and dad are gone. In the exercise, the stakes are small, but the revelations can be very big. There are few things more important to the long-term success of your family than having different personalities, like a child who's a highly skilled and successful professional and a sibling who has chosen a career in the arts or as a stay-at-home parent learn to work together and appreciate each other's input and opinions. With an eye toward the long term and a little patience, through a system of trial and error and a spirit of cooperation, your kids will discover they can achieve something big and positive together. Occasionally, the upshot of this exercise is the realization that certain family members are not able to work together, which gives the parents the opportunity to either assist with a child's further development, or make appropriate adjustments to the estate plan.

10. Enlist the Help of Mentors— Especially Family Elders.

We all know the saying, "If you give a man a fish, he'll eat for a day; but if you teach a man to fish, he'll eat for a lifetime." As a parent, the philosophy provides an apt comparison of the difference between telling your kids what to do and helping them figure it out for themselves. Giving great advice is all well and good, but enabling your children to wisely self-advise is priceless.

Mentoring is the ultimate form of guidance, unique from teaching and coaching in that it accomplishes the greater goal of helping people figure out *their own* solutions. It's an art form, really: asking just the right questions, with the implicit understanding that the answerer has the solution within himself or herself. The questions just make it easier to find. The fact of the matter is that no advice is ever as useful or perfect as that answer within. One of my own mentors, co-founder and CEO of The Heritage Institute, Rod Zeeb, says, "If you tell somebody something, it's an opinion. But if they come up with it themselves, it's a fact." How true that is!

As a parent, you can certainly mentor your own kids, but look around and ask yourself who else can serve this role for your family, perhaps to mutual benefit. Grandparents, aunts and uncles, trusted advisors, and friends—these are people who usually have tremendous experience and wisdom. Many times they are right there, sitting on the sidelines of your life, an older generation underutilized and withering on the vine. Talk with these people about being available to mentor the rising generation of your family. They may well be able to help your heirs internalize some of the important principles on this list. Furthermore, these relationships will be some of the most cherished your heirs will have in their lives, and elders often find fulfillment and purpose in helping the rising generation. It's a win-win for your entire family.

11. Start Now.

Start to plan and prepare your heirs for their transition as early as humanly possible—like today. Whether your "child" is six or 60, the time to work through potential inheritance issues is sooner rather than later. Waiting until you come face-to-face with circumstances that remind you of your own mortality will put undue pressure on your family to race through a process that inevitably takes time. Worse yet, if you don't work with your children to prepare for the future, you could leave them to cope, unprepared, with the full gamut of emotions—grief, confusion, fear, isolation, resentment, insecurity, euphoria, distrust—that come with the loss of a parent, coupled with an inheritance they aren't prepared for.

CHAPTER 8

Preparing Your Estate

When you've accomplished good communication, mutual respect, coordination, and trust in your family, then it's time to come back to your existing estate plan and ask yourself, *What do I want this to look like now? What do we need to modify so that our planning reflects our family as it is now, serves our highest aspirations for them, and supports the legacy we're really trying to create?*

In most cases, after going through the process of reaching their place of possibility, parents find that their previous estate plans no longer reflect the way the family functions or the future they envision for the rising generation. Typical, traditional estate plans are designed to be as defensive, preventive, and protective as possible. Unfortunately, these plans can backfire, with heirs fighting among themselves, suing to break trusts, and resenting the structures that were designed to protect them.

What should the nuts and bolts of estate planning look like for your thriving family? It's a very personal decision with countless options, but there a few guidelines that may help you to create a plan that is in line with the inclusive, supportive, positive changes you've brought about in your family.

Don't Put Your Faith in Restrictive Trusts

Trusts with distributions based on age, academic achievement, career milestones, marriages and childbirth, and even vaguely identified "meaningful pursuits" are almost certainly doomed to fail. Again and again, I've counseled grown children who are so stunned and hurt by the construction and negative nature of these trusts that they have lifelong ramifications. Kids have told me, "I can't believe my dad's last act was to make sure I couldn't touch his money. Why didn't he trust me?"

All too often, these kinds of trusts end in ugly litigation to break the trust. One need look no further than the massive Rollins family fortune and its ongoing legal debacle to see the potential harm. The heads of the family entrusted with managing the trusts for this Atlanta-based clan have been accused of not just withholding distributions because third-generation heirs aren't engaged in what they deem to be "meaningful pursuits," but also of adding stipulations to the trusts that allow them to use investigators to check on their children's progress and dig through medical and other personal records. The heirs, not surprisingly, are fighting back, and the family has been very publicly and painfully torn apart in the fallout.

There very well may be legitimate reasons to rely on restrictive trusts to preserve your family's wealth, but I recommend you only use them as a last resort. If you do, you should have an open and honest conversation with your heirs about the limitations and the reasons for them. The damage these types of trusts can cause is far worse when the heirs are unprepared for them than when they know the restrictions are inevitable.

Consider an Alternate Trust Structure

There are times when, despite your best efforts, it becomes apparent that an heir is not ready or able to inherit. In these cases, there is a kind of trust that doesn't rely on controlling the beneficiary's behavior to succeed. Instead, Financial Skills Trusts (FST) or Results-Oriented Trust Environment (ROTE) plans offer a more fluid trust structure that simply requires the beneficiary demonstrate basic financial skills—with no arbitrary dates, milestones, or achievements spelled out as "proof" of that accomplishment. In the case of and FST or ROTE, the beneficiary typically has to demonstrate he or she can live within his or her own means—in other words, spend less than comes in; save a portion of their income; be able to understand and successfully manage credit and debt; be able to reasonably maintain an accounting of finances; and be able to generate additional income when desired—for example, with a second job. When these conditions are met, the trust can authorize distributions to the beneficiaries. The structure allows for quite a bit of discretion by the trustee to help the beneficiary accomplish his or her goals.

While not ideal, this trust is a way of saying, "We're not going to contribute to your demise by giving you money if it's going to create dependency and make your life worse. So you've got to be living in a way that meets your basic needs and not overspending—*in any way that works for you*—to receive this inheritance."

Separate Personal Belongings from Your Estate

So many families get pulled apart by fights over personal belongings. Mom's sapphire ring has much more emotional pull than a comparable amount of money in a bank account. Rather than lump your personal possessions in with your estate, if something matters to you—or you think it will matter to your children—create a separate, detailed, and clear Personal Property Memo to explain your preferences. Better yet, write personal letters to accompany personal items.

Don't Leave Any Debts or Debtors Behind

If you have loaned money or given gifts that might be construed as loans to your heirs, make a clear designation as to any debts or debtors in your estate plan. Do not leave your family squabbling about whether one sibling's down payment or wedding expenses constitute a debt that must be repaid to the estate.

Keep Things Even, or Explain Yourself

Nothing is more toxic to a family and its legacy than parental favoritism. No one issue can tear up a family faster than having siblings discover they have not been treated equally in a parent's estate plan. People often equate love with money, so unequal distributions are perceived as being loved more or less in the recipients' minds. Sadly, I've witnessed this painful and divisive event in my own family. Even mature and loving brothers and sisters can get psychologically knocked right back to the "He got more!" mentality of childhood by unequally divided bequests. If you feel you must treat children unequally in your estate plans, know that they may fall out with one another as a result. At the very least, have a personal conversation with everyone affected to explain your reasons. This is something that absolutely has to be done face-to-face, not in a letter your attorney reads after you're gone.

Don't Saddle the Next Generation with Your Dreams

No matter what wonderful things you accomplished in your life—and no matter how proud your kids are of those accomplishments—please don't expect your family members to devote their futures to the same endeavors, charities, causes, properties, hobbies, and/or people you have loved, after you are gone. Be sure your estate plan gives your heirs enough freedom to be able to choose their own careers, their priorities, and their own causes.

Prepare Trustees and Executors

Preparing your heirs includes making sure your executor, successor trustee, or family business manager is both willing to serve and understands what it means to do a good job in those vitally important roles. Preparation includes teaching the entire family what it means to be a good beneficiary and a good trustee. Trustees can be so much more than just gatekeepers keeping heirs from their money—a great trustee will help teach and mentor the beneficiaries just like the parents would do if they were still in the picture. And a well-trained beneficiary will understand and appreciate the role and the challenges the trustee has to deal with. These understandings can make all the difference in assuring a smoothly functioning trust.

Assemble a Cooperative Support Team

Once you've begun making progress creating your own thriving family experience, it's a great time to introduce your kids to your advisors, and your advisors to your kids. Doing this as part of a family meeting is ideal. Make sure everyone involved appreciates the role the others play. Create an opportunity for your trusted financial and legal advisors to explain what they do and how their actions protect the family's assets. This is also a great time to have them begin to provide educational opportunities for the family to learn more about financial management, budgeting, tax, and estate planning issues.

This opportunity benefits everyone involved. Your kids meet the people you trust to manage your family's wealth and affairs, and the advisors have the opportunity to connect with the people who will ultimately be deciding the future of the family's estate.

In the unlikely event that you have an advisor who resists this opportunity, or who pushes back against your less defensive estate plan, think long and hard about whether you want this person to be in charge when it comes time to administer your estate plans. In my experience, many advisors—and certainly the best advisors— are comfortable with and prefer working with other advisors as part of a collaborative team working in your family's behalf.

THE MOST IMPORTANT THING

Anyone who has worked with me in a professional capacity has heard me say, "The failure to talk to the kids sows the seeds of the family's demise." Failure to communicate is the biggest, most ominous, most dangerous threat to your estate plan and to your family's long-term success. And so, once you've got your estate plan in order, you have one more critical and difficult step to take: You must have an open and frank discussion with your family, in which you outline the details of your estate plan.

Let's just be perfectly candid about this event: No one wants to do it—not you or anyone else in your family—but it may be the single biggest kindness you can offer your heirs with regards to your estate. I tell my clients that like it or not, this is the event for which parents must summon their courage, pull themselves up by their bootstraps, and get on with it. As difficult as it is to endure what you might call a "pre-reading" of your will, it is one key to keeping small and large estate decisions from festering and eventually blowing up and causing irreparable harm to the family unity that you have worked so hard to create.

The best way to proceed is to hold a family meeting, preferably in a neutral location, guided by your estate attorney or another appropriate and neutral professional facilitator. Before the meeting begins, identify any potential trouble spots in your estate plan that might be cause for concern with one or more of your children. Consider how you will address those concerns in a way that is consistent with your overarching desire to continue creating a thriving family experience. If you need professional help to assure this goes well, hire a professional facilitator.

With your family present, speak to your family first about your love and concern for them, their well-being, and family togetherness after you are gone. Tell them how much thought and effort you have put into your planning, and that the plan you have come up with isn't necessarily perfect, but it does balance your desires with your vision for the long-term best interests of your family. Share your wish that everyone understand your thinking, and your knowledge that this does not mean you think everyone in the family will agree with you on every point. Then, have your attorney start at the beginning, "Point One of the estate. Your father/mother wants . . ." and then review your preferences and plans, point by point, with your heirs all in the room.

Why should you go through this process? This is your one opportunity to be crystal clear about your wishes—to share the facts; take questions; and explain what you want and *why* in a safe and sheltered environment where *you*—the one person with the answers—can do any damage control that's needed. How many parents, if they had to witness the reading of their wills and the fallout in their families, would give anything just to have one more chance to offer a few words of explanation, or of compassion, or of reassurance?

I think of my client whose kids turned right around and handed his life's savings over to a con artist; I think of the parents of a woman who swore she'd never go back to her family home again after learning the terms of her mother's restrictive trust; I think of my own father, and the hurt his well-intentioned but unequal bequests wrought in our family. They could have alleviated so much suffering if they'd just had a chance to explain.

The discomfort of this event is the price you have to pay to ensure that your wishes are clear, that your family members understand them, and that they know your choices are made with love, good will, and hope for a lasting family legacy of prosperity and togetherness. If you've gone through the steps in this book, you'll get through it just fine, and your family will be better off for the time, trust, and love you've put into the process.

CONCLUSION

It was Emily Dickinson who wrote the beautiful line, *I dwell in possibility.* The work my team and I do with families is all about promise, potential, and reaching that place of possibility where a family is thriving—connected, communicating, celebrating their shared past, and working together to better the causes and populations they care about.

When all those things are happening, and when a family's elders are brave and wise enough to look ahead and wonder, "What will keep us together?" then they can create not just an inheritance of wealth and worldly goods, but an inheritance of history, purpose, vision, love, and hope. That's the kind of magic I hear in *possibility.*

My colleagues and I are committed to slashing the 90 percent failure rate of the *shirtsleeves* proverb to 50 percent over the next 20 years. What a difference that would make, not only to the families themselves, but also to the wider world. Think of the power of the increased philanthropy of all those families—the wells that could be dug, the deaths from treatable diseases that could be prevented, the babies who could be vaccinated, and the school children who could go home to a hot meal every night. The good that thriving affluent families can and will do is nearly limitless.

It is my sincerest hope that this book enables you and your family to heal damaged relationships, curb destructive behaviors, and transition from feuding to flourishing in the process. As you reach that thriving family experience, I hope you find it brimming with the magic of possibility, with the promise of family unity, and with the knowledge that your family has been blessed not just with the gifts of the here and now, but with the long-term security and grace of your lovingly nurtured endless inheritance.

ACKNOWLEDGEMENTS

I cannot begin to thank my beautiful and amazing wife Ingrid Del Monte for everything she has meant to me in life. She has been the one who loves me unconditionally; she convinced me to go into private practice in 1992 despite my nagging doubts; she was my first business partner; and she has always been "the one" I have relied on above all others for love, guidance, and unwavering support. She's able to see everything that I miss, and without her by my side, I would be utterly lost. She means everything to me.

My five children—Mark, Megan, Eryn, Richie, and Tori—have given me so much joy, laughter, and purpose in life, and their happiness and success in life is supremely important to me. I love them all dearly, and am so happy I get to be their Dad.

I would never have been able to achieve the level of joy and satisfaction I have experienced serving families if not for the constant optimism and encouragement, and the amazing talent, brains, and firepower of my business partner, Angela Wright Baumsteiger. She moves mountains like they are specks of dust, and I'm grateful for her many, many vitally important contributions to this book.

Thanks are also due to Jana Murphy, my writing partner for this book. Her insights, wisdom and perseverance have been crucial to this book's success.

I also appreciate the contributions and support of my editor-in-chief, Patti "Yes We Can" Boysen.

I'm also grateful for the support of my business coaches and advisors, including Jennifer Summer Tolman, Tracy Beckes, Kurt Wright, Jack Beatty, and Dan Sullivan of Strategic Coach. They have each blessed me with vision, and instilled in me the burning question, "If not me, who? If not now, when?"

I'm extremely thankful for the great contributions of Rod Zeeb, CEO of The Heritage Institute, and all my colleagues there. It was Rod who first opened my eyes to the possibility of helping families avoid what he calls The Midas Curse. My life has never been the same since. I'm also indebted to Mitch Harris, CEO of The Heritage Institute UK, for his valuable contributions and wise counsel.

Of course, every professional stands on the shoulders of those who came before him, and I am so thankful for the contributions of the true pioneers in the field of creating thriving families, including James E. "Jay" Hughes, Jr., Charles Collier, and Roy Williams.

Speaking of being carried on others' shoulders, I want to thank the phenomenal members of our firm's great staff over the years, including Jeff and Jennifer Gurnett, Michelle Drury, who is our resident empath, and Chris Hughes, whose skill in wealth management has given me space to write, teach, speak, and, of course, help families thrive.

I'm also in awe of the contributions of my fellow founding members of the Council for Shared Leadership, including Jennifer Summer Tolman, Lee Brower, John Dankovich, Courtney Pullen, Barb Culver, Rod Zeeb, David Parks, Charlie Haines, Jr., Tim

Belber, Scott Farnsworth, Kristin Keffeler, Mike Cummins, David Cohn, and Ron Nakamoto. You can see the pioneering contributions these giants have made to the cause of creating thriving families at www.thrivingfamilyexperience.com. Another hero of mine is John A. Warnick, the founder of the Purposeful Planning Institute.

I also want to thank some of the individuals in my life who have inspired, mentored, believed in and helped me on my journey, including Jim Greenan; Paul Clark; Darrell Wiley; Gregg, Jerrilyn, Colette and Dan Ankenman; Sal Sbranti; Nate Lincoln; my 108-year-old uncle Bill Del Monte and his amazing niece Janette Barroca; my uncle and aunt, Jack and Francine Del Monte; all my other aunts, uncles and grandparents who have passed on; my wonderful cousins, who I love to death; my mother, Mary Del Monte; and my brother and sister, Pat and Kelly Del Monte. Also, Jerry Boucher, Paul Cowell, Mike Reed, Harry Milhisler, Jeff and Terrie Hart, Steve Hotze, Jonathan Mandel, Paolo Monti, Les Proceviat, Patty Ruiz, Banafsheh Ahklaghi, Carol Gallagher, Nate Baumsteiger, Keith Weinstein, Marybeth Viglione, and, of course, Deborah Joy. Every one of these brilliant folks has played a crucial role in my life and my career.

Most important of all, I would like to thank the Lord for placing me here in this, the most amazing time in history, and for giving me the talents, abilities, relationships, and opportunities that have allowed me to grow, develop, and make a meaningful difference in the lives of others.

Richard Del Monte

December 2014

ABOUT THE AUTHOR

RICHARD M. DEL MONTE is a Certified Wealth Consultant and nationally recognized expert on the subject of families and wealth. Richard has appeared on FOX Business News and has been featured in *The Wall Street Journal, The New York Times, Private Opportunities Club, Private Wealth Magazine, Trust & Estates,* and *Family Wealth Report.* A sought-after speaker, he recently gave a TEDxBellevue talk titled, "A Place of Possibility for Families and Wealth."

Clients seek guidance from Richard to help create more positive relationships between family members and with money; to mentor the rising generations around how to avoid destroying inherited wealth—or letting it destroy them; to offer guidance on passing on values to heirs; and to ensure the family's wealth lasts for multiple generations. Richard's road-tested advice helps self-made families deal with the complexities of wealth transfers with ease and grace. Best of all, he teaches his client families teamwork tools they can use to foster closer relationships, more effective communication, and achieve greater satisfaction in their lives.

In addition to receiving the CFP®, CWC, and MBA in Financial Planning designations, Richard has completed specialized training in family dynamics and preparing heirs. He holds an MBA in Financial Planning from Golden Gate University and a

BS in Business Administration from California State University, Chico. He is a faculty member at the Institute for Preparing Heirs, and is a founding member of the Council for Shared Leadership, LLC, which established fundamentals of excellence for values-based advisors and the families they serve.

Richard lives in Alamo, California, with his wife Ingrid, two of their five children, and their three golden retrievers. Richard's community activities include participation in the United Way of the Bay Area, John Muir Health Foundation, Boy Scouts of America, and his church. He also serves as an advisor for Barag-wanath Blessings, a Bay Area-based charity with the mission of helping babies and children in need around the world.